The Trivia Lovers'
Guide To

GOLF

The Trivia Lovers' Guide To

GOLF

First published in 2007
Reprinted in 2009

Acknowledgement
In an earlier edition of this book material was used from the section 'Origin of Golf Words and Terms' on the website of Scottish Golf History, which was the copyright of Scottish Golf History. Complete Editions fully acknowledges Scottish Golf History's copyright in that material. Readers interested in accessing the site for this and additional information should visit: www.scottishgolfhistory.net

Packaged by Susanna Geoghegan HP2 6HG
Cover and design by Peter Wilkinson
Typeset by David Onyett, Publishing & Production Services, Cheltenham
Printed in China

Introduction

Mark Twain may have dismissed golf as 'a good walk spoiled', but millions of golfers the world over would surely take issue with the celebrated American writer. Golf may be the cause of a certain amount of frustration at times, as accounts in the pages that follow indicate; but it has also been a source of endless fascination for players and spectators since its early days, when Scotsmen (and certain notable Scots women as far back as the 16th century) perfected the art and guile of hitting a small ball into a far-off hole.

Golf has many attractions, not the least of which being that it is a game enjoyed by players of almost any age – here you'll find the exploits of players aged under ten and approaching 100. Golf is also a game in which one simple action is honed and perfected to an art of sublime dexterity and infinite variety. Perhaps the truly amazing feature of the game is the manner in which the world's leading players have been, and are, able to sustain a level of supreme performance week in, week out, for year after year over a wide variety of courses and climatic conditions, as this book shows.

From details about the evolution of the game, its famous courses, players and the equipment they use, to remarkable feats from tee to cup, by way of the fairway, bunker and the occasional transgression into the rough – this book is packed with golfing facts and figures, anecdotes and achievements. As the great Arnold Palmer once observed, 'Golf is legends and lore, great images and greater vision.' And who could argue with him?

GOLF

Open for Golf

There were three rounds played over 12 holes at the inaugural Open, and only eight players were invited to take part in the contest, which began at noon and ended by dusk on the same day. There was no actual prize money and participants had to pay their own travelling expenses. Hosts Prestwick Golf Club in Ayrshire did, however, pay £25 for a fine red leather and silver belt (the Challenge Belt) which became the trophy for the winner.

The idea for the competition had been around for a few years. To begin with, Prestwick had approached two east-coast clubs – The Honourable Company of Edinburgh Golfers and the Royal and Ancient Golf Club of St Andrews – with the proposal that they should join forces to stage a 36-hole stroke competition to be held at venues on a rotational basis. However, after the other two clubs had failed to commit to the idea, Prestwick decided to go it alone and held the first competition in October 1860. When the championship was staged the following year, it was declared open to the whole world and it has stayed as such ever since.

The championship was held annually at Prestwick for 11 years during the course of which the outstanding Young Tom Morris took permanent possession of the Challenge Belt after a hat-trick of victories in 1868,

1869 and 1870. (The first hole-in-one scored at the Open was claimed by Young Tom Morris on his first round in the 1868 championship, playing the 166-yard 8th hole at Prestwick.)

After a year's abeyance, the Open was staged again, this time with the assistance of the two clubs Prestwick had approached initially. The three clubs shared in the purchase of a new trophy, which is still is use today. Tom Morris won the championship again in 1872, as a result of which he became the only player to win the Open four years running.

Over the next two decades the Championship was held on the clubs' three courses: Prestwick, Musselburgh (which the Honourable Company of Edinburgh Golfers shared with other clubs) and the Old Course at St Andrews. In 1872, it was staged at Muirfield, which had become the home of the Honourable Company, and the championship was extended to 72 holes.

Further changes followed two years later, when the championship moved south of the border for the first time, to be staged at Royal St George's, in Sandwich, Kent. The Royal Liverpool Golf Club at Hoylake joined the group of courses holding the Open, and before the First World War the Royal Cinque Ports course at Deal was added to the list.

GOLF

Scoring Terms

Ace	Hole in one shot
Deuce	Hole in two shots
Albatross	Three under par for the hole
Double Eagle	(as above) Three under par for the hole
Eagle	Two under par for the hole
Birdie	One under par for the hole
Par	The number of strokes considered necessary to complete a hole or course in expert play
Bogey	One over par for the hole
Double Bogey	Two over par for the hole

Three out of Fifty

That was the rather dispiriting success rate of British PGA teams in the first 50 years of the Ryder Cup. The three occasions on which they did win were: at Moortown, Leeds in 1929, at Southport and Ainsdale in 1933, and at Lindrick, Yorkshire, in 1957; and never in the United States.

Even when a European team replaced the British PGA team it suffered three consecutive defeats before beating the Americans at the Belfry in 1985 and again in the United States two years later (the first time that an American team had been beaten at home in the Ryder Cup).

Young Driver

In 2001 Jake Paine of Lake Forest, California, grasped his driver and teed off. His ball flew and rolled and plopped directly into the cup for a hole-in-one. At 48 yards, the distance of the hole he was playing may not have made his feat among the most memorable in the history of golf. What was undeniably impressive, however, is that young Jake was only three years old at the time.

Pebbles and Rabbit Holes

One popular theory is that the modern game of golf originated with fishermen on the east coast of Scotland. They would apparently amuse themselves as they walked home to the village from their boats by using pieces of driftwood to knock pebbles along among the sand dunes. It's even possible the idea of a 'hole' as the final destination of the ball – or pebble – came from the object falling down a rabbit hole.

Banned by Royal Proclamation

There were many golf-like games throughout Europe dating from medieval times. These include *jeu de mail*, *pell mell*, *crosse* and *kolven*. One game was called *cambuca*, which seems to have been similar to the game of *paganica*, which was from Roman times. *Paganica* was played with a bent stick that was used to strike a leather ball stuffed with feathers.

In *cambuca* the stick or club was curved and the ball was also stuffed with feathers. *Cambuca* was certainly played in England in the 14th century, and was one of the sports banned by a royal proclamation in 1363 in a bid to encourage archery practice. There is a window in Gloucester Cathedral which depicts a headless figure swinging a club at a yellow ball. The illustration dates from the 14th century and is thought to be of someone playing *cambuca* – though the figure is generally known as the 'golf player'.

One-Day Open

The first US Open was played over a nine-hole course at Newport, Rhode Island, in 1895 and was won by English player Horace Rawlins with a score of 173 over the four rounds. The event started and finished on the same day. Rawlins, who was an assistant professional at the course, won prize money of $150, and received a $50 gold medal. Just eleven people entered.

Air Shots

In 1905 the pioneering manufacturer of golf balls, B. F. Goodrich, introduced a revolutionary product to the rapidly growing golf market. This was the pneumatic ball, filled with compressed air, which could be driven further than any other ball in use at the time. Regrettably, it contained one insurmountable design problem which prevented it from achieving its full marketing potential. The pneumatic ball had the unnerving tendency to explode in hot weather.

In the Bag

The first golf bags were developed from around 1885, and were often wicker baskets or containers made of canvas. Before their introduction, golfers either got their caddies to carry the clubs – or carried the loose clubs themselves under their arms. Some club carriers at this time were in the form of a tripod so that the bag could be placed on the ground in an upright position.

British Open Roll of Honour

Most Victories   6 – Harry Vardon, 1896, 1898, 1899, 1903, 1911, 1914

Second-Place Finishes   7 – Jack Nicklaus, 1964, 1967, 1968, 1972, 1976, 1977, 1979

Largest Margin of Victory   13 strokes – Old Tom Morris, 1862

GOLF

Lowest Winning Score   267 – Greg Norman, Royal St George's, 1993

Lowest Round   63 – Mark Hayes, 2nd round Turnberry, 1977

Oldest Winner   Old Tom Morris, 1867, 46 years 99 days

Youngest Winner   Young Tom Morris, 1868, 17 years 5 months 8 days

Most Consecutive Wins   4 – Young Tom Morris, 1868–72 (tournament not played in 1871)

Most Top-5 Finishes   16 – J. H. Taylor, Jack Nicklaus

Wire-to-Wire Winners   Ted Ray, 1912; Bobby Jones, 1927; Gene Sarazen, 1932; Henry Cotton, 1934; Tom Weiskopf, 1973

Fourball and Foursomes

Not to be confused, fourball and foursomes are two distinctive ways in which competitive golf are played.

In a fourball competition two players form one team to play against another team of two players. The best scores on each hole by each team are counted to make up the team's total score.

In a foursome competition, there are again two players on each team, but each team plays with just one ball. In America this type of competition is known by the more easily understood term 'alternate shot'. As this suggests, the players on a team take it in turns to play the ball. Each of them tees off alternately as well, irrespective of who played the last putt on the preceding hole.

Understanding Fairways

'Fairway: a narrow strip of mown grass that separates two groups of golfers looking for lost balls in the rough.'
Henry Beard and Roy McKie

Open Play-Offs

Until 1963 play-offs for the title in the British Open were decided over 36 holes. That year, the New Zealand left-hander, Bob Charles, won the title after a play-off with the American, Phil Rogers.

Golf Club Selection

Writing at the end of the 19th century, the Scottish golfing champion Robert Chambers listed the selection of clubs that every well-equipped player should have to hand They were:

- The 'play club' for driving
- The 'mashie' or 'long spoon' for getting out of roughs
- The 'short spoon' for short drives of 100 yards or less
- The 'brassie', a wood with a protective brass sole
- The 'sand iron' for lofting the ball out of hazards and over stymies
- The 'cleek', an iron for long shots
- The 'niblick' or 'track iron', a small club with a heavy iron head made for getting the ball out of holes

One club that Chambers omitted to mention proved to be of great value to golfers in the days before motor cars. This was the appropriately named 'rut iron', designed specifically to chip a ball out of the rut formed by a wagon wheel. The arrival of pneumatic-tyred motor vehicles and the banning of traffic from crossing golf courses spelt the end of this invaluable addition to the golfer's arsenal.

Dunlop 65

For many years the Dunlop 65 was probably the best-known golf ball in Britain. It evolved as a result of a shrewd piece of marketing by the manufacturer whose ball had been used in the 1934 Open Championship held at Royal St George's. This was the championship in which the winner, Henry Cotton, hit a new record score for the event: 65 in his second round. The new Dunlop golf ball was brought out to record his triumph and remained popular with golfers for decades.

Illegal Action

In 1895 the USGA banned the use of billiard cues for 'putting' golf balls. This decision was brought about following a dispute during the US Amateur Championship.

In 1968, 73 years after billiard cues were banned, it was also ruled illegal to hit a ball by standing astride it and striking it with the action of a croquet mallet.

The Presidential Line

The Walker Cup, contested between amateur teams from the United States and Great Britain and Ireland, was first played in 1922. The competition is named after George Herbert Walker, President of the United States Golf Association in 1920, who donated the trophy. His maternal grandson was also a president − George Herbert Walker Bush: the 41st President of the United States of America. The 'W' in the name of George W. Bush, the 43rd President, also stands for Walker.

The competition was originally and formally known as the United States Golf Association International Challenge Trophy, but the media found this a little long-winded and were soon calling it the Walker Cup. The first match was played at the National Golf Links of America on Long Island and was won by America.

At Arm's Length

To drop a ball in golf, players are meant to hold it at arm's length and then let go. At one time, however, they were supposed to drop it over their shoulders. This requirement was eventually dropped because too many balls dropped in this way were bouncing off players' bodies and rolling some distance away.

A Stamp of Success

The victory of American amateur Francis Ouimet in the 1913 US Open at Brookline, Massachusetts, is often seen as a crucial moment in American golf. Ouimet, who came from an ordinary working background, had to ask for time off work to compete in the tournament. His win, in which he fought his way back from behind to beat two British professionals, Harry Vardon and Ted Ray, caught the imagination of the US public – and helped transform the image of golf from being a sport for the rich to one for all Americans, of all backgrounds. Ouimet became the first American to be made captain of the Royal and Ancient Golf Club in 1951. And in 1988 a US stamp was issued to commemorate the 75th anniversary of Ouimet's US Open win.

Lightning Report

The first qualifying day of the 1936 Open Championship was washed out by torrential rain and a violent thunderstorm shortly after lunch. One news agency reporter was relaying his story by telephone to London when a bolt of lightning struck the phone lines outside the press tent at the auxiliary qualifying course at Wallasey, surged down the wire to the receiver he was holding and flung him across the tent. Instead of reporting the news, the shaken reporter found himself making it when his colleague from Hoylake interviewed him on how it felt to be struck by lightning at the Open Championship.

Overenthusiastic Fans

Gary Player twice fell foul of adoring fans in the space of just two years. In 1962 the vigorous handshake from one fan sprained his hand and cost him the tournament and two years later, when he was competing in the US Open a crowd of autograph hunters accidentally pushed him into a water hazard.

GOLF

Keep It Simple

'I have always believed there are far too many rules in golf. For me, if you cannot write them all on the back of a matchbox then something is wrong.'

Henry Longhurst

Illegal Play

By the middle of the 15th century golf was already so popular in Scotland that the parliament of King James II passed a law which made playing the game illegal, on the grounds that it was distracting Scotsmen from practising archery, which was regarded as an essential part of national defence in the event of war with England.

Anyone caught playing golf was either fined or imprisoned. In spite of this the game remained popular, particularly among noblemen who enjoyed playing golf on links courses by the sea. The arrival of gunpowder later in the century made battlefield archers obsolete and in time the ban was lifted and golfers were free to play a round free from the risk of legal punishment.

New Business

It is estimated that around 400 new golf courses open in the USA every year.

Stroke of Misfortune

A little under a century ago a competitor in the qualifying round of the Shawnee Invitational for Ladies in Pennsylvania teed off at the 118m (130yd) 16th hole and found herself in more than a spot of bother. Unluckily for her, the ball sailed from the tee directly into the Binniekill River, where it bobbed to the surface and began to make its way downstream. Undeterred, the redoubtable competitor took to the water herself, in a rowing boat, with her husband at the oars, and set off in pursuit of her golf ball.

After perilous attempts to retain her balance while striking the ball, she succeeded in bringing it to land 2.4km (1.5 miles) downstream. This was not the end of her difficulties, though. Between her and the 16th hole lay a wood, through which she had to play her ball until finally sinking her closing putt. From tee shot to final putt, that hole had cost her 166 strokes.

Getting the Blues

Golf clubs were formed at both Oxford and Cambridge universities in the mid-1870s. At Oxford, the land surrounding a college cricket pitch was brought into use to serve as a makeshift golf course. However, golf was restricted to times of the year when cricket was not being played, which ruled out much of the best weather of the year and at least one whole term.

GOLF

When it came to playing the inaugural golf match
between the two universities, their two golf clubs settled
on the Wimbledon course of the London Scottish club.
Four singles matches constituted the event and Oxford
emerged victorious in all of them.

Swinging in the Rain

'The difficulty of the rain was that you could not see.
The rain was coming down horizontally and every time
I looked up to see where I was going, it hit me in the
face and stung.'

> Greg Norman, describing the weather conditions
> he faced when hitting a round of 74 to win his
> first British Open in 1986

Sibling Rivalry

The winner of the 1891 British Open was Hugh
Kirkaldy , with his brother Andrew finishing in second
place – the first time two brothers had shared the top
spots in the event. They came from a poor background,
sons of a miner who had fought in the Crimean war.
Andrew Kirkaldy, himself a soldier, was the 'nearly' man
of the Open – he was three times runner-up, and
finished in third place three times and fourth place twice.
But sadly, he never won it. In the 1889 Open he came,
literally, within an inch of the title at Musselburgh but
missed the simplest of one-inch putts. This led to a

play-off with Willie Park Jnr – which Kirkaldy lost. In later life he was made honorary professional of the Royal and Ancient.

Bunkers for Ever

The great Bobby Jones had set views on what was correct on the golf course – and what wasn't. He once explained his preference for traditional terminology, saying: 'I use the word "bunker", meaning a pit in which the soil has been exposed and the area covered with sand. I regard the term "sand trap" as an unacceptable Americanisation. Its use annoys me almost as much as hearing a golf club called a "stick". Earthworks, mounds, and the like, without sand, are not "bunkers".'

The Opening Twelve

The original Open Championship at Prestwick was held over these 12 holes:

1	Back of Cardinal	578 yards
2	Alps	385 yards
3	Tunnel (Red)	167 yards
4	Wall	448 yards
5	Sea Headrig	440 yards
6	Tunnel (White)	314 yards
7	Green Hollow	144 yards

8	Station	166 yards
9	Burn	395 yards
10	Lunch House	213 yards
11	Short	132 yards
12	Home	417 yards

The Open Championship ceased to be played at Prestwick after 1925 when the size of the crowds drawn to watch the event made the layout of the course unsuitable for the increasing number of spectators.

Aiming High

The world's highest golf course used to be the Tuctu Golf Club at Morococha in Peru, which lay 4,369m (14,335ft) above sea level, although Timothy J. Ayers played a shot from the summit of Mt McKinley in Alaska at an altitude of 6,194m (20,320ft). Today, La Paz Golf Club in Bolivia has the highest regularly played golf course in the world at a height of around 3,341m (10,800ft).

Let Battle Commence

'The golfer has more enemies than any other athlete. He has fourteen clubs in his bag, all of them different; 18 holes to play, all of them different, every week; and all around him is sand, trees, grass, water, wind and

143 other players. In addition, the game is 50 per cent mental, so his biggest enemy is himself.'

Dan Jenkins

Botanical Collection

Each hole of the Augusta course is named after plants, trees or flowers which grow on the course. These are:

1st	Tea Olive
2nd	Pink Dogwood
3rd	Flowering Peach
4th	Flowering Crab Apple
5th	Magnolia
6th	Juniper
7th	Pampas
8th	Yellow Jasmine
9th	Carolina Cherry
10th	Camellia
11th	White Dogwood
12th	Golden Bell
13th	Azalea
14th	Chinese Fir
15th	Firethorn
16th	Redbud
17th	Nandina
18th	Holly

(The 11th, 12th and 13th holes at Augusta were named Amen Corner by golf writer Herb Warren Wind, who reckoned the power of prayer was needed to get players through them without problems.)

The Sticky Postage Stamp

The eighth hole at Royal Troon is called the Postage Stamp after its tiny green flanked by three bunkers. This was the hole that proved the undoing of German amateur Herman Tissies, when he competed in the 1950 Open. He managed to rack up a score of 15 for the hole as he played his ball from bunker to bunker – taking five shots in one of them – before finally landing on the green where he needed three putts before finding the cup.

That 1950 Open also saw the use of an experimental rule that reduced the penalty for an unplayable ball to distance only. In one round, the eventual runner-up, Argentine golfer Roberto de Vicenzo, exploited this rule to his advantage when his ball landed in one of the bunkers guarding the eighth hole. Claiming that the ball was unplayable, Vicenzo returned to the tee for a second attempt and this time succeeded in landing the ball close enough to the cup to hole it with a short putt to score par three for the hole. That experimental rule was subsequently removed from the game.

The eighth hole at Troon also featured in the 1973 Open in which the 1932 champion, Gene Sarazen competed to mark the 50th anniversary of his appearance in the event. Playing the Postage Stamp in his first round, Sarazen scored a hole-in-one and came very close to doing the same thing in the second round.

Hitting the Treble

The sixth hole at Carnoustie was once extolled by Gene Sarazen who commented to an interviewer, 'I believe that the sixth hole at Carnoustie, played against the wind, is the nearest approach to a perfect par five in the world.'

In 1953 his fellow American, Ben Hogan was preparing for the Open on the same course. After two practice rounds, he approached he sixth hole on his third. After hitting a drive, Hogan asked for his caddie's assistance, giving him specific instructions: 'I am going to hit three long iron shots from here to the green, one to hit the ground on the left front of the green, the next at centre front and the third at right front. I want you to tell me exactly how each ball bounces, and in what direction, after it touches the ground.'

The caddie did as he was asked: positioned himself on the green and watched Hogan hit his three long iron shots precisely as he had predicted.

GOLF

Clubhouse Trophy

The trophy for the US Masters tournament in Augusta was introduced in 1961, and is designed after the old colonial clubhouse at the course. The trophy is engraved with the winner's name, while the winner himself receives a smaller replica.

All Wright

Mary Kathryn Wright – better known as Mickey Wright – won an amazing 13 events out of the 32 she entered in 1963. The Californian-born player won four US Women's Open titles in her brief but glittering career, which was cut short by injury.

Canada Rules the World

The World Cup was started in 1953, but until 1966 it was known as the Canada Cup. It was the idea of Canadian businessman John Jay Hopkins and the first tournament was held in Montreal. The competition is an international event for professional players, with two golfers taking part from each competing country. There is also an individual prize for the player with the lowest score. The inaugural 1953 event was won by Argentina, with Argentine player Antonio Cerda winning the individual prize. The first tournament was held over 36 holes.

Unexpected Birdie

A freak of golfing bad luck brought national chaos to the West African state of Benin when the country's air force was destroyed. The culprit, as far as the authorities were concerned, was golfer Mathieu Boya, who had been practising on open land next to the Benin air force base, since there were no golf courses in the country at the time. Nothing was amiss until one of Boya's shots smacked into a flying bird, which flopped downwards and dropped straight into the cockpit of a fighter plane that was about to take off. The unexpected arrival of an injured bird in his lap caused the pilot to lose control, and his jet piled into four other Mirage jet fighters parked nearby. As a result of the crash, all five planes, valued at a total of $40million, were written off. That was the entire Benin Air Force. Boya may have considered himself a trifle unlucky, but was put in jail anyway for his errant drive.

Three's a Crowd

Apart from being a good player, Archie Compston was also something of an eccentric. He was not content with just one caddie, but instead had three. One carried Compton's clubs, another his other kit such as spare clothes, and the third was on hand to keep the Englishman topped up with cigars, cigarettes or his pipe.

GOLF

According to the Rules

The first known Rules of Golf were drawn up in 1744 by the Gentlemen Golfers of Edinburgh, who would go on to become The Honourable Company of Edinburgh Golfers, for the world's first open golf competition held at Leith.

Articles & Laws in Playing at Golf.

1. You must Tee your Ball within a Club's length of the Hole.

2. Your Tee must be upon the Ground.

3. You are not to change the Ball which you Strike off the Tee.

4. You are not to remove Stones, Bones or any Break Club, for the sake of playing your Ball, except upon the fair Green and that only within a Club's length of your Ball.

5. If your Ball comes among watter, or any wattery filth, you are at liberty to take out your Ball & bringing it behind the hazard and Teeing it, you may play it with any Club and allow your Adversary a Stroke for so getting out your Ball.

6. If your Balls be found any where touching one another, You are to lift the first Ball, till you play the last.

7. At Holling, you are to play your Ball honestly for the Hole, and not to play upon your Adversary's Ball, not lying in your way to the Hole.

8. If you should lose your Ball, by its being taken up, or any other way, you are to go back to the Spot, where you struck last, & drop another Ball, And allow your adversary a Stroke for the misfortune.

9. No man at Holling his Ball, is to be allowed, to mark his way to the Hole with his Club, or anything else.

10. If a Ball be stopp'd by any Person, Horse, Dog or anything else, The Ball so stop'd must be play'd where it lyes.

11. If you draw your Club in Order to Strike, & proceed so far in the Stroke as to be bringing down your Club; If then, your Club shall break, in any way, it is to be Accounted a Stroke.

12. He whose Ball lyes farthest from the Hole is obliged to play first.

13. Neither Trench, Ditch or Dyke, made for the preservation of the Links, nor the Scholar's Holes, or the Soldier's Lines, Shall be accounted a Hazard; But the Ball is to be taken out teed and play'd with any Iron Club.

John Rattray, Capt

For the best part of two centuries these rules were thought to have been lost until they were discovered on the last two pages of the Honourable Company's Minute Book. The pages contained the original thirteen Articles and the signature of John Rattray, the first winner, who was 'Captain of the Golf' 1744–1747 and 1751.

In those days golf was only a match play game, which explains some of the wording in these early rules. A decade after they were drawn up by the Edinburgh club, they were adopted by the newly formed Royal and Ancient Golf Club of St Andrews. However, by this stage Rule 5 had been amended. Where it had originally stated that when a ball was removed from 'watter or any wattery filth', it was to be brought 'behind the hazard and teeing it', the amendment established the procedure of 'throwing it behind the hazard 6 yards at least, you may play it with any club', thereby removing any reference to requiring players to tee up the ball.

Clubbing Together

The earliest golf clubs were made by bow makers, carpenters or wood-turners and their club-making skills were passed down from generation to generation. There is a record of the Scottish court paying a bow maker in Perth 14 shillings for making a set of clubs in 1502. Another document records the king's treasurer having to pay out 14 shillings for a bet the king lost with the Earl of Bothwell over a game of golf.

Professional Approach

When Mike Reasor injured his left arm in a riding accident, he decided to play on and finish the last two rounds of the Tallahassee Open in 1974 using just one arm. Not that Reasor figured he could still win the event – as his scores of 123 and 114 testify. But he was smart enough to know that as long as he completed the tournament, he would win automatic entrance to the next PGA tour event.

The End of the Small Ball

Two different sizes of golf ball were in use for almost 60 years. The 1.68 in (large ball) was the standard in use in North America, while the 1.62 in (small) ball was used in the rest of the world, though was illegal in North America.

At the beginning of 1990, however, an announcement from the Royal and Ancient Golf Club sounded the death knell for the small ball: 'With the steady and, in most countries, rapid decline in the use of 1.62 in ("small") ball the R & A has been considering changing to the 1.68 in ("large") ball for some time, but has held off from doing so mainly because of the large number of Japanese golfers still using the small ball. With the use of the small ball in Japan now dropping steadily, and in most other countries now being at 10 per cent or less, it seems an appropriate time to make this change.'

Cayman Golf

When Jack Nicklaus and his colleagues were commissioned to construct a golf course on the small Caribbean island of Grand Cayman, they could not find enough open ground for the right price for a full-size course. The solution? Build a smaller course – about 4,000 yards smaller.

In order to make this playable, they had the inspired idea of requiring golfers to use short-range balls: ones specifically designed to travel only half the distance of conventional golf balls. Playing with balls that are driven just 140 yards down a fairway for example, matched the reduced dimensions of the new course and introduced to the sport what Nicklaus dubbed 'Cayman

Golf', as a result of which several other half-size courses have been built.

The Greatest Among Them

The first professional golfer to achieve real public recognition in his own lifetime was Allan Robertson, who was born in St Andrews in 1815 and died, aged just 44, in 1859.

At his death one of the members of the Royal and Ancient Golf Club commented that the 'greatest among them is gone'. Robertson's grandfather had been a professional golfer and also a ball-maker, while his father had been an accomplished golfer too. It was accepted that Robertson was the best golfer of his time and such was his reputation that it was even believed by some – though this was not the case – that he had never lost a game of golf. He was, however, the first player to go round the Old Course at St Andrews in under 80 shots: a feat he accomplished in 1858.

Ironing Out the Wrinkles

'My golf swing is a bit like ironing a shirt. You get one side smoothed out, turn it over and there is a big wrinkle on the other side. Then you iron that one out, turn it over and there is yet another wrinkle.'

Tom Watson

GOLF

Battling in the Bunker

Bunkers can be more than just a golfing hazard. In
1931 D. Bayly MacArthur was playing at Rose Bay,
New South Wales, when his ball flopped into a bunker.
The burly MacArthur got in to play a rescue shot – but
soon needed rescuing himself. Recent heavy rain had
turned the sand into the kind of quicksand you see in
old Tarzan films. By the time his desperate cries for
help were heard, MacArthur was up to his elbows and
only just got out in time.

Signing Away the Money

Jacqueline Pung missed out on her best-ever chance to
win the US Women's Open when in the 1957 event
she headed the field – but was then disqualified for
signing an inaccurate scorecard. The title was awarded
instead to second place Betsy Rawls. The financial blow
for Pung of missing the prize money was, however,
softened when a sympathetic golf writer organised a
collection for the player which raised $2,500 – $700
more than the winner of the tournament received.

Royal Partner

Before James II of England (VII of Scotland) followed
his brother, Charles II, to the throne, he became
involved in a golf challenge match with two English

noblemen. The match was to be played over the Links at Leith, and Prince James had the good sense to invite a poor shoemaker named John Paterson to play as his partner, because Paterson was reputed to be a very fine golfer. This proved to be the case and the prince and his partner won the match. Prince James generously gave all the prize money to Paterson who used it to build a house; as a shoemaker with royal patronage, his business flourished as well.

Snead on Match Play

The great Sam Snead had ten maxims for success at match play. They were:

1 Play more conservatively early in the match.
2 When in doubt, check your opponent's lie.
3 After winning a hole, concentrate on hitting a solid drive.
4 When the momentum is going against you, change the pace of the match.
5 Always figure your opponent will make (a long putt).
6 Never give up on yourself.
7 Don't get mad; get even.
8 When you decide to gamble, 'Katy, bar the door.'
9 Know the rule differences for match play.
10 Always keep the pressure on your opponent.

GOLF

Overseas Victor

The first non-British player to win the Open
Championship was the French golfer, Arnaud Massy,
who was victorious at Hoylake in 1907. Massy had
competed in the event for several years before winning
it and in the two years prior to his success he had
finished tied for fifth place and sixth.

Ladies on the Links

The earliest recorded reference to a woman playing golf
dates from 1568, when Mary Queen of Scots was
reproved for playing golf near Musselburgh after her
husband, Lord Darnley, had been murdered.

Musselburgh was also the setting of the first known
reference to a woman's golf competition, which was
played in January 1811. The Ladies' Golf Club at St
Andrews was established in 1867 and the following year
the one at Westward Ho! in Devon was formed. In
both these cases, however, women golfers played on
putting courses; it wasn't until the 1870s that women
began to play with a set of clubs on short courses.

Golf: a Definition

As late as the closing years of the 19th century the
majority of Americans were more than a little confused

about the game of golf, as an explanatory article published in the *Philadelphia Times* illustrated:

'It is sometimes agreed that the game shall be won by him who makes the largest number of holes within a given number of minutes, say 20 or 30 ... each player places his ball at the edge of the hole designated as a starting point. He then bats it ... toward the next hole. As soon as it has started he runs forward ... and his servant, who is called "caddy", runs after him ...'

Judgement by Eye Only

Apart from accepted optical aids, glasses and contact lenses, golfers are forbidden from using any other devices to enhance their vision or assist their estimation of distance from a hole. So, binoculars, telescopes, range-finding equipment, global positioning systems and similar devices are all ruled ineligible on the golf course.

An Ace for Ike

US President Dwight D. Eisenhower, who took office in 1953, was a keen player though he did not take up the game until he was 37 – possibly because his duties as a rising army officer left little time for recreation, though it is interesting to speculate whether or not he considered that being President of the United States of America afforded him greater free time.

Eisenhower played more than 800 rounds during his tenure in the White House and even had a putting green constructed on one of the lawns. He often played at Augusta National and once managed a very respectable 79 on the course. A pine tree there is known as the Eisenhower Tree because the president hit it so often – though the course administrators thankfully refused his presumably light-hearted suggestion that they cut it down.

His greatest golfing moment came in 1968, when Eisenhower was 77, and just a year before his death. The then former president and one-time Supreme Commander of the Allied Expeditionary Forces in Europe during the Second World War said it was the 'thrill of a lifetime' when he holed-in-one at the Seven Lakes Country Club in Palm Springs.

With a Little Help From Your Friends

The famous Ryder Cup victory by Great Britain and Ireland over the United States in 1957 at Lindrick was the last time that Britain and Ireland ever beat the Americans. They lost every match from then until 1979, when fellow European players were invited in to bolster the team. Even then the Europeans had to wait until 1985 and their historic win at The Belfry. The 1957 team was captained by Welshman Dai Rees. The 1985 team was skippered by non-playing captain Tony Jacklin.

Unprofitable Sportis

In 1491 the Scottish Parliament of King James IV passed a statute which ordained that 'in na place of the Realme there be used Fute-ball, Golfe, or uther sik unprofitable sportis', on the grounds that they detracted from 'the commoun good of the Realme and defense thereof'.

This last point was of particular importance. The authorities had become increasingly concerned that skill at archery (on which the nation depended in large measure for security on the battlefield) was being sacrificed for skill at golf; men were spending too much time playing golf and too little time practising archery.

It wasn't only early golfers who could be said to have threatened national security in this way. In the late 15th century Scottish bowmakers were developing a tidy sideline making golf clubs alongside their more conventional output. Paradoxically, the king himself is known to have bought 'Gowf clubbes' from a bowmaker in Perth.

Bouncing Back

'The only equivalent plunge from genius I can think of was Ernest Hemingway's tragic loss of the ability to write. Hemingway got up one morning and shot himself. Nicklaus got up next morning and shot a 66.'

Ian Wooldridge, on Jack Nicklaus's start to the 1981
Open at Royal St George's, at Sandwich, when he hit
81 in the first round and the next day completed the
course in 15 fewer strokes to qualify

In the Swing

'"My swing is too fast" may be the biggest mis-
conception ever. Think about it. If you take a fast,
lousy swing and slow it down, all you've got left is a
slow, lousy swing. Most people swing too slow, not too
fast.'

Hank Haney (swing coach to Tiger Woods)

The Business of Golf

Business Golf Strategies, a company that instructs
businesses on how to sell on the golf course, has broken
down the average round of golf into distinct marketing
phases.

The first four holes are designated for building rapport
with the client. The next ten holes, from five to fifteen,
are for talking business. After that the advice from
Business Golf Strategies is to drop the business chat and
concentrate instead on making sure that your client is
having a good time.

Only at the 19th hole should you bring the conversation round to business again. That is when you should go for the kill.

A Lot of Bottle

Playing in the 1949 British Open, Harry Bradshaw suffered the misfortune of driving his ball into a beer bottle, breaking off the neck and shoulder. This left him with two options: play the ball where it lay (inside the half-broken bottle), or take a penalty and move it. Bradshaw decided against the penalty, smashed the bottle with his club and sent the ball a further ten metres.

Bradshaw then finished in a tie for first place with Bobby Locke of South Africa, only to lose to him in the 36-hole play-off.

All the 9s

R. H. Corbett's score of 27 on the first nine holes at a course in England in 1916 consisted of nine consecutive scores of 3, including two eagles.

Wind Assistance

One of the longest drives ever seen in the Open was hit by Craig Wood in the 1933 tournament on the Old

Course at St Andrews. Wood's drive on the par 5 fifth hole, helped by a strong tail wind, went some 430 yards. Wood was rewarded for his big-hitting that year with second place.

Natural Hazards

Golfers playing the Jinja course in Uganda are permitted to follow a couple of local rules that are not found on many other golf courses.

If a ball lands near a crocodile, for example, and the player decides that playing it is unsafe, another ball may be dropped, so that that can be played.

Similarly, if a ball lands in a footprint made by a hippopotamus, it may be lifted and dropped without penalty.

Golf International

Friends Simon Clough and Boris Janjic played five rounds of golf in one day in 1992, each of them in a different country: France, Luxembourg, Germany, the Netherlands and Belgium. Airline executive Alain Reisco was even more adventurous when he managed a round in three different continents on the same day – playing in Morocco in Africa, Spain in Europe and the United States in the Americas.

The Masters

The first winner of the US Masters tournament in 1934 was Horton Smith with a round of 284. The winner of the tournament when it was first officially called the Masters in 1938 was Henry Picard. The first non-American to take the title was the South African Gary Palmer, who won in 1961 – the first of three Masters championships for him. Seve Ballesteros was the first European to win the US Masters, in 1980, while the first Briton was Sandy Lyle in 1988. Remarkably, Britons then won the Masters for four consecutive years: Lyle again in 1988, Nick Faldo in 1989 and 1990 and Ian Woosnam in 1991.

South America

The tenth hole at Carnoustie is called South America. It was named in honour of a young caddie who had a few drinks too many in the clubhouse one night. The youngster boldly declared he was off to make his fortune in South America. The next morning, however, the lad was found sleeping it off – by the 10th hole. It's been known as 'South America' ever since.

Unholy Places

'When that happens [the demise of golf], old men will furtively beckon to their sons and, like fugitives from the guillotine recalling the elegant orgies at the court of Louis XV, will recite the glories of Portmarnock and Merion, of the Road Hole at St Andrews, the sixth at Seminole, the eighteenth at Pebble Beach. They will take out this volume from its secret hiding place and they will say: "There is no question, son, that these were unholy places in an evil age. Unfortunately, I had a whale of a time.'"

Alistair Cooke, from his foreword to
The World Atlas of Golf

End of the Royal Line

While presidents and prime ministers may enjoy an easy, if at times intensely frustrating, relationship with golf, the same cannot be said of kings and emperors. Here are some of the golf courses associated with them that are no more:

Royal Baghdad – closed after 1958
Royal Bombay, India – closed 1947
Imperial Country Club, Tehran, Iran – closed after 1979

Ministerial Sanction

Arthur Balfour, who became Prime Minister in 1902, was a keen golfer and was captain of the Royal and Ancient Club in the 1890s. His passion for the sport is regarded as having helped the popularity of the game at a time when some criticised it. A prominent magazine in 1886 had suggested that only stupid people played golf. The fact that someone as highly regarded as Balfour – then Chief Secretary for Ireland – played the game helped to defuse such attacks.

Birdies of the Wrong Variety

Golfers in Australia are known to complain about crows and indigenous black birds called currawongs, that swoop down and steal golf balls while they are being played. On one occasion a bird's nest was blasted with a water cannon and 40–50 stolen golf balls came tumbling out from it.

Hell's Half Acre

This is the name of the world's largest bunker, which forms one of the hazards at the Pine Valley golf course in Clementon, New Jersey. This enormous bunker stretches 100 yards along the hole.

Golf Train

In order to reach the tee on the 11th hole of the course at Golf de Sainte-Maxime, near St Tropez in southern France, players have to take a funicular railway.

GOLF

Which Club?

The average golfer will hit a ball approximately these distances with these clubs:

CLUB	MEN (yards)	WOMEN (yards)
1-wood	225–235	175
2-wood	215–225	
3-wood	210–215	153
4-wood	190–200	
7-wood	175–185	109
9-wood	160–170	
11-wood	145–160	
1-iron	195–200	
2-iron	190–195	
3-iron	180–190	130
4-iron	170–180	120
5-iron	160–170	110
6-iron	150–160	100
7-iron	140–150	90
8-iron	130–140	80
9-iron	120–130	70
Power Wedge	110–120	55
Sand Wedge	100–110	44

Trainspotters

The first hole at Prestwick is situated on the other side of a wall from Prestwick railway station and runs alongside that wall. Local lore holds that one golfer sliced his tee shot at the first hole, sending it over the wall to land on a goods train that was trundling by. By all accounts his ball eventually came to rest in Glasgow.

On another occasion the hole was being played as the 19th hole in a club foursome match when both the drive and second shot from one pair bounced back into play after striking the railway track. From the second of these rebounds the ball landed four feet from the cup, resulting in the pair winning the hole and the match with a birdie three, in spite of the fact that they had technically been out of bounds on two occasions.

Leading by Example

Baudoin I King of the Belgians is unique among European monarchs in having played golf for his country. He first played in an international competition in 1958 – in a three-way match with France and the Netherlands.

180 Not Out

In 1874 a member of the Aberdeen Golf Club announced that he would undertake to play a dozen rounds of golf on the 15-hole Aberdeen links course and then walk a distance of ten miles – and all within one 24-hour period. Sure enough, on 6 July 1875, club records noted, 'This day Mr Bloxham appeared to play the twelve rounds and walk the ten miles he backed himself to do at the last dinner. He began work at six in the morning and finished his twelve rounds between 8 and 9 pm. He afterwards walked from the first milestone on the Deeside road to the sixth at Milltimber and back to the Schoolhill, where he arrived at about 1.15 am, thus triumphantly performing his task with some hours to spare.'

In the course of playing his 180 holes of golf, Bloxham had walked approximately 32 miles across the links. Despite this, he was playing well enough on his final round that he was able to concede a stroke a hole to his opponent, the club secretary, and still beat him by 14 holes, with only the final hole being halved.

Prior to this achievement on his home course, Bloxham had played 16 rounds of the 9-hole course at Musselburgh, against the professional and three times Open champion, Bob Ferguson. That match also started at 6 am and finished 11 hours later at 7 pm.

A Tale of Two Countries

Llanymynech Golf Club, which sits on the English–Welsh border, is unique for at least a couple of reasons. This is the course where a nine-year-old tyro named Ian Woosnam learned to play golf. It's also the only course in Europe where you can play one round of golf in two countries: 15 of the holes are in Wales, the other three are across the border in England. And playing the fourth hole you cross the border, teeing off in Wales and putting out in England.

Do Not Disturb

'The least thing upsets him on the links. He misses short putts because of the uproar of butterflies in the adjoining meadows.'
P. G. Wodehouse, on a highly sensitive golfer

Innovations of the Year

At least three innovative developments in golf equipment were made in 1996. A company in San Rafael, California, began marketing the catchily named Peace Missile Golf Clubs, made from melted-down Soviet nuclear missiles.

In the same year a resident of Houston, Texas, patented a telescopic device to go inside golf holes. When a putt is sunk, this ingenious contraption automatically raises the ball high enough to let the golfer collect it without having to bend down.

Another 'labour-saving' gadget produced in 1996 was a revolutionary golf club fitted with a small explosive detonator in the head. This, the manufacturers claimed, was capable of firing a golf ball considerably in excess of 280 yards without great effort on the part of the golfer. Enterprising, and no doubt potentially popular as this might have been, the USGA moved quickly to ban it from tournament play.

Starter for Ten

The Irish golfer Christy O'Connor took part in no fewer than ten Ryder Cup matches between 1955 and 1973.

Locke Down

Bobby Locke, the great South African player who won the first of his four British Open titles in 1949, had a strict upbringing in the sport. Locke, who had a handicap of 14 by the time he was eight, was warned by his father that if he didn't learn to keep his bad temper under control while playing golf he would have the boy's clubs taken away for ever.

Locke was regarded as one of the greatest putters the sport has seen. In 1945 the South African did not three-putt on a single green, though he played about 1,800 holes that year. It was said that Locke was so fond of his putter that sometimes he slept with it.

Aces High

Playing in the 1971 Martini Tournament at Royal Norwich, John Hudson teed off on the 11th hole and was understandably delighted to find that he had struck a hole-in-one. After this lay the par four 12th hole. Again, he readied himself on the tee and, again, to everyone's astonishment, the ball flew majestically towards the green, landed and rolled into the hole to score a consecutive ace.

At the end of the round, however, Hudson's total of 72 placed him ninth to Bernard Gallacher.

Verse and Worse

In spite of achieving the remarkable feat of winning both the US Open and US Amateur titles in the same year, 1916, Charles 'Chick' Evans had previously played in seven US Amateur competitions without winning one of them.

In the face of his lack of success, Evans even set his apparent inability to win the title in verse, though fortunately for him, his downbeat assessment was to be proved wrong. All the same, the sentiments he expressed will be all too familiar to many golfers:

I've a semi-final hoodoo, I'm afraid

GOLF

I can never do as you do, Jimmy Braid.
I've a genius not to do it,
I excel at almost to it,
But I never can go through it, I'm afraid.

Pipped at the Post

'Golf is not like tennis, or basketball, or football where
you can control your opponent. With golf you cannot
control your opponent. If Jack [Nicklaus] misses a
couple of putts I win the tournament. But he didn't, did
he? We did!'

Tom Kite, airing his admiration and frustration
when both he and Greg Norman were
overhauled by Jack Nicklaus, who went on to
win the 1986 US Masters that Kite and
Norman were both poised to win

Export Business

By the mid-18th century the business of making golf
clubs and golf balls had become well established in
Scotland. Over a century before playing golf was
considered to have begun in America, records from
Scottish ports show that Scottish golf clubs and golf
balls were being exported to the colonies. Between 1743
and 1751 almost 1,000 balls and 168 golf clubs were
exported to Virginia and South Carolina from the Port
of Leith. In 1765, records from the Port of Glasgow

show that 144 golf balls and 18 golf clubs were exported to Maryland.

Lucky 13

Sometimes a player finds a course really to their liking. Joe Lucius scored his 13th hole-in-one at the 15th hole at the Mohawk Golf Club in Ohio in 1984. He had already achieved ten holes-in-one at the 10th hole.

Here's Mud in your Eye

Mark Calcavecchia was forced to pull out of the Kemper Open in 1986 in Maryland after he hit his ball into a ravine. The problem wasn't hitting the ravine, or even the lie of the ball; it was that Calcavecchia fell into a huge muddy puddle clambering down to the ball and was so covered in mud he couldn't continue.

Against the Odds

While shaving on the morning of the final round of the 1941 US Open Craig Wood strained his back bending to pick up the razor he had dropped. So great was his discomfort that he could only compete wearing a truss, in spite of which he still managed to win the title.

American golfer, Phil Mickelson, broke both his left leg and right ankle in a skiing accident in 1994, and recovered to maintain his place among the leading golfers of his generation.

Ed Furgol won the US Open in 1954 even though he had a withered left arm.

Forty years earlier, Yves Botcazou, the assistant at the Versailles course of Golf de la Boulie, very nearly qualified for the 1914 Open at Troon, although he had no left arm.

Eighty years after his achievement, Ray Woodhouse became one of a special group of golfing 'aces', when he hit a hole-in-one at Mapperley Golf Club, Nottingham, in May 1994. He, and the small band of golfers he joined, managed this even though he too had only one arm.

A Tranquil Frame of Mind

'When Braid, Taylor and I were much-of-a-muchness, and playing together frequently in exhibition matches, we were always desperately keen to beat one another. Golf is not a game at which one dare slacken, even in a friendly game. Only, if you play rounds every day at high tension for two or three weeks before a championship, you are very likely to lose your zest through sheer staleness. Somebody has said that golf is "nine-tenths mental". The estimate is not far wrong.

For that reason, training which involves compliance with regulations that are irksome is apt to be a bane rather than a blessing to your game. For this game you need, above all things, to be in a tranquil frame of mind.'

Harry Vardon, writing in *Golf Monthly* in 1921

Disqualified

In 1992 the Zimbabwean golfer, Nick Price, was disqualified from playing in the Million Dollar Challenge at Sun City, South Africa, because he moved an advertising hoarding.

Severiano Ballesteros was disqualified from competing in the US Open in 1980 after he arrived ten minutes late on the tee and still wearing street shoes.

Johnny Bulla was also disqualified from the US Open (in 1941 in his case). This time the offence was teeing off early.

In 1981 the Dutch player Constant Smits van Weasberghe was disqualified from the 1991 European Tour for incorrectly replacing a ball.

Vijay Singh was similarly disqualified from the Asian Tour for adjusting a scorecard.

GOLF

White House First

William McKinley, who became the 25th President of
the United States in 1897, was the first incumbent of
the White House to play golf.

Featheries

Until the middle of the 19th century golf was played
with leather balls stuffed with feathers. (Reputedly, as
many feathers as could fill a top hat were packed into a
single golf ball.) Costly to make, these suffered in wet
weather, when they lost their shape. They were also
vulnerable to splitting if mishit, especially by an iron
club. These limitations aside, 'featheries' flew well in
dry conditions and Samuel Messieux once succeeded in
driving one 361 yards at St Andrews: an outstanding
achievement given the equipment available to golfers in
the 1830s.

Writing sixty years later, H. Thomas Peter observed in
Reminiscences of Golf and Golfers, 'The making of first-class
feather balls was almost a science. The leather was of
untanned bull's hide: two round pieces for the end and
a strip for the middle were cut to suit the weight
wanted. These were properly shaped, after being
sufficiently softened, firmly sewn together (with a waxed
linen thread) – a small hole of course left, through this
little hole the leather itself had to be turned outside in,

so that the seams should be inside. The skin was then placed in a cup-shaped stand, the worker having the feathers (from the breast of a goose or chicken) in an apron in front of him, and the actual stuffing done with a crutch-handled steel rod (known as a brogue), which the maker placed under his arms. And very hard work, I may add, it was. Thereafter the aperture was closed and firmly sewn up: and this outside seam was the only one visible.'

Wartime Rationing

Rubber balls were in short supply during the war. At the 1945 Los Angeles Open, Sam Snead used just one ball during the tournament. It was given to him by Bing Crosby. Though the cover had got a little loose by the end, Snead still won the event.

In wartime South Africa there was a Wooden Golf Ball tournament, won by A. A. Horne who banged and rattled his way round the course to win with a very respectable score of 90.

A Lot of Bottle

When he was a youngster, Lee Trevino used to bet players at his golf course that he could beat them playing with a Dr Pepper bottle taped to a stick. Several took him on and several lost their bets.

GOLF

Where Eagles Dare

So close and yet so far, so very far. Poor Bruce Devlin looked in contention for the Andy Williams San Diego Open at the Torrey Pines Golf Course in 1975. With just one hole to play, Devlin was only two shots off the lead and went for a huge second shot in search of the eagle he needed. Unfortunately the ball sank into a water hazard and it took the luckless Devlin seven shots to get out. In the space of just one hole he had slipped from third to thirtieth spot in the tournament.

Lunar Golf

In 1974 the US Golf association museum in Far Hills, New Jersey, received a unique addition to its collection. This was the Spalding six-iron with which Alan Shepard, Commander of the Apollo 14 spacecraft, had hit two golf balls on the surface of the moon; one of which, according to Shepard, 'went for miles and miles and miles'.

Acknowledging his unique feat, the R & A sent Shepard a telegram, which read, 'Warmest congratulations to you and your colleagues on your great achievement and your safe return. Please refer to Rules of Golf section on etiquette, paragraph 6, quote, before leaving a bunker a player should carefully fill up and smooth over all holes and footprints made by him, unquote.'

Threes-in-One

Most golfers feel hugely satisfied if they hit a hole-in-one directly from their tee-off. However, there are some who manage every golfer's dream the hard way.

One of the strangest holes-in-one was achieved by John Remington at a course in England in 1959. The ball landed in a bunker, bounced off a length of drainage pipe, hit a nearby rake, flew up onto the green, and careered into another ball – before finally disappearing down the hole.

In 1981 Ted Barnhouse teed off on a par three hole at Mountain View, California and watched in dismay as his ball sailed over a fence into a nearby field. All was not lost, though. The ball struck a grazing cow on the head, richocheted off her skull on to a lawnmower and bounced off that onto the green where it smacked into the flag and dropped into the hole.

Back Nine – the Wisdom of Bobby Jones

1. Many shots are spoiled at the last instant by efforts to add a few more yards.

2. Nobody ever swung a club too slowly.

3. The best exercise for golfers is golfing.

4. I have a tip that will take five strokes off anyone's game. It's called an eraser.

5. I never learned anything from a match that I won.

6. Too much ambition is a bad thing to have in a bunker.

7. You swing your best when you have the fewest things to think about.

8. The moment the average golfer attempts to play from long grass or a bunker, or from a difficult lie of any kind, he becomes a digger instead of a swinger.

9. A leading difficulty with the average player is that he totally misunderstands what is meant by concentration. He may think he is concentrating hard when he is merely worrying.

Never on a Sunday

The Church in late 16th century Scotland took a dim view of people playing golf on a Sunday. So much so, that repeated offences could lead to excommunication. Evidence from 1599 shows that at St Andrews a person who played on the Sabbath would be fined for the first two offences, before eventually facing harsher punishment.

Keeping Up With Jones

Between 26 May and 27 September 1930 the American golfer Bobby Jones accomplished the unique feat of winning the Open and Amateur golf championships of both Britain and America

At the end of May, Jones won the British Amateur title at St Andrews, commenting afterwards, 'I could take out of my life everything except my experiences at St Andrews and still have a rich, full life.' Three weeks later, between 18 and 20 June, he was victorious in the British Open at Hoylake, on the Wirral. Less than a month later (between 10 and 12 July) he was playing in the US Open at Interlachen, Minneapolis, which he also won. Lastly, between 24 and 27 September Jones won the US Amateur title at Merion.

The story about the first of Jones's 1930 victories has become part of golfing legend, if only for the fact that the change of rules which removed a stymie from the game meant that no one will ever win a match as Jones did. The draw for the competition placed Jones against Cyril Tolley, the defending champion and twice winner of the event, in an early round. Eagerly anticipated, this encounter was regarded by many as the match of the decade – of the century, some maintained.

Both players ensured that they lived up to expectation.

With never more than one hole in it, they arrived at the 17th hole of the Old Course at St Andrews, where Jones holed from eight feet to stay on level terms. The 18th hole was also halved and the match moved to the 19th. There Tolley mishit his shot to the green and followed this with a weak chip that left his ball seven feet from the hole in three. Jones, on the other hand, was ten feet away in two strokes and on the same side of the green. Jones putted first and his ball stopped two inches from the edge of the hole, directly in Tolley's line of approach. As Jones later commented, the hole was totally cut off to anything but a miracle and this dead stymie won him the hole and the match.

Cyril Tolley was gracious in defeat, accepting that his weak chip had left him at the mercy of a stymie, though Jones acknowledged his regret that a match of such quality had been decided in that way. As history would show, the fates were with Bobby Jones that summer and shortly after achieving his win at Merion, he retired from the golf circuit to devote himself to his law practice; although he did found the Augusta National course.

After the Augusta course was finished in 1934, Bobby Jones organised an invitation event that year for top players. The original suggestion for the name of this event was the 'Masters Tournament' but Jones rejected this as too 'presumptuous'. So it was called the Augusta

National Invitation Tournament, until finally in 1938 Jones gave way over the name and it became known as the Masters.

Long Odds

The odds of hitting a hole-in-one have been estimated to be 1 in 8,606, which works out at one hole-in-one for every 478 full rounds of golf played.

Being Gene Sarazen

Gene Sarazen – who was born Eugenio Saraceni – became the first player to win the US Open and the USPGA in the same year, when he picked up both titles in 1922. He was only 20 years old at the time. He had originally left school to work as a carpenter, but was advised to take up an outdoor career for health reasons. So Sarazen became a caddie. It was the unlikely start of a great golf career.

Sarazen changed his name in 1918 after seeing it printed for the first time in a newspaper – he'd just hit a hole-in-one at a course in Connecticut. Sarazen said he looked at the name 'Eugenio Saraceni' and decided it sounded more like a violin player than a golfer. He chose Sarazen because he couldn't find anyone else with the same name.

GOLF

Woods

A variety of different woods were traditionally used to make clubs. The heads were often made out of fruitwoods, thorn wood and beech; though the most efficient was found to be persimmon, which had to be imported from the Americas. The shaft of the club was made out of ash, hazel and other woods until hickory was found to be the best choice both for strength and the straightness of the grain.

Sponsorship

In the inter-war years and for a time after the Second World War, virtually all the professional golf tournaments held in Britain were sponsored either by golf ball manufacturers or by national newspapers. So tournaments bore the names of golf balls such as Dunlop, Penfold and Silver King, or the names of newspapers: *Daily Mail*, *News Chronicle*, or *News of the World*. The latter's match-play tournament which began in 1903 came to be recognised as the match-play championship of the Professional Golfers' Association. Sponsorship by the *News of the World* ended in 1968.

Book Learning

Larry Nelson, who won his first US Tour tournaments in 1979, and who later won the US Open once and the

USPGA twice, took up golf very late in life for a professional. Nelson was 21 before he first hit a golf ball and apparently learnt all his golf from a book.

Odd Balls

Golf balls struck in tournaments have come to rest in some unlikely places, though few have been stranger than these.

Playing at the Sea Pines Heritage Classic, Hale Irwin played a shot that sent the ball merrily on its way to come to rest in a spectator's bra.

Bobby Jones once managed to hit a ball into an abandoned shoe that was sitting inside a parked wheelbarrow.

Cary Middlecoff, the Tennessee golfer who won the US Open twice, the US Masters once (in 1955) and who was also a qualified dentist, once lost a tournament through a bizarre chain of events. Middlecoff was leading the field when he hit his ball into the pocket of a spectator. The spectator panicked, threw the ball into the rough and ran away. Middlecoff double-bogeyed the hole and lost the tournament as a result.

One of the more unusual shots in golf history was made by the wonderfully-named Aubrey Boomer at the St

GOLF

Anne's Golf Course in Scotland in 1923. Somehow
defying the laws of physics, Boomer, a fine player who
was runner-up to Bobby Jones in the 1927 Open,
managed to hit the ball straight up in the air. And
when the ball came down it landed neatly in Boomer's
right pocket.

A Stroke of Bad Luck

Roberto de Vicenzo missed out on the chance to win
the US Masters in 1968 thanks to a simple scoring
error by his playing partner Tommy Aaron at the 17th
hole. Aaron mistakenly put down de Vicenzo for a par
4 instead of the birdie 3 he had really shot. De Vicenzo
didn't spot the mistake and after the round signed for a
66 – when he really had gone round in 65.
Unfortunately for the Argentinian, the carded score had
to stand, and he missed out on a play-off with eventual
winner Bob Goalby by that one stroke.

Steady as you Go

Dale Larson suffered what might be termed a golfing
accident at a golf course in Wausau, Wisconsin, and
successfully sued the club for $41,000 in damages.
Larson's counsel claimed that he had slipped while
wearing his golf spikes because the surface he was
walking on was brick. Had Mr Larson been walking on
concrete, the attorney asserted, he would not have

fallen onto his face and thereby incurred the need for major dental work.

Fortunately for his client, the jury agreed that the golf course was 51 per cent responsible for the injuries Dale Larson had suffered, while he was 49 per cent responsible. This decision was reached in spite of the fact that the injured man tottering around in golf spikes had consumed 13 drinks that evening.

Golf Ball Innovations

For centuries golf and related games had been played with leather balls packed with feathers, but in 1848 a new material was brought into use that revolutionised the manufacturing process. This was a black rubber-like substance known as gutta percha. Softened in hot water, it was shaped into a ball, heated again and compressed as much as possible and then put in cold water to harden.

New balls made from gutta percha did not carry as far as featheries, though golfers began to notice that they flew further once they had acquired nicks or indentations from being struck by golf clubs. So manufacturers started marking the surface of their gutta percha balls, initially by hammering them and later with the use of moulds and machines.

Although gutta percha balls would only at best fly as far as featheries, and had little bounce when they landed, they lasted far longer than feather-filled balls and were significantly cheaper. By the 1870s other materials were mixed with gutta percha to produce composition or gutty balls.

The Rules of Golf according to Watson

'There are only two basic rules that matter. One: play the ball as it lies. Two: if you don't know what to do next, do what you think is fair.'

Tom Watson

Cutting Edge

In 1829 the world's first hole-cutting tool was brought into service at the Musselburgh links, near Edinburgh. Holes were cut on greens there for the next 64 years without attracting much comment or interest (except from players who failed to direct their balls accurately in their direction). Then, in 1893, the Royal and Ancient Golf Club of St Andrews ruled that golf holes throughout the world should all be the same size and the standard model prescribed was the holes at Musselburgh. These happened to be 4.25 inches wide and this has been the diameter established for the cup on golf greens the world over ever since.

The Hole Truth

In playing on the green
Though rivalry be keen
With courtesy for ever fill your role;
Antagonists may gain,
Yet kindly you'll refrain
From talking till the

> ball
> is
> in
> the
> hole

Though warm may be the day
And hot the game you play,
Yet you should keep as cool as Arctic pole;
Let others fret and fume,
The calmest air assume
And keep it till the

> ball
> is
> in
> the
> hole

'Golf' printed in *The Elgin Courant Courier*,
Christmas Eve, 1895

GOLF

The Best Medicine

The demanding but beautiful Royal Troon Club in Ayrshire was founded in March 1878, largely at the instigation of a local doctor, Dr John Highet. The first meeting to set up the club was held at a local pub, the Portland Arms Hotel. The club emblem has a serpent encircling a set of clubs – the serpent represents medicine and is a reference to the professional background of its founder. The club motto is a good one for those who believe in brain as much as brawn in the sport: 'Tam Arte Quam Marte' ('As much by skill as by strength'). The club was called Troon Golf Club until it received its Royal Charter on its centenary in 1978.

Stymied on the Green

Until 1951, when a change was made to the rules of golf, a player could be stymied on the green if his opponent's ball lay on his putting line to the hole. Players were only allowed to have an opponent's ball lifted while the putt was made if the two balls lay within six inches of each other. (For this reason score cards were six inches wide to provide a handy measure.)

The rule permitting a ball to be lifted stated, 'When balls lie within six inches of each other on the putting green (the distance measured at the nearest points) the ball lying nearer to the hole may, at the option of either the player or the opponent, be lifted, until the other ball is played.'

If the two balls lay more than six inches from each other, then the player making the putt had to negotiate his opponent's ball either by attempting a lofted shot over it or by trying to play a curling shot around it.

In 1951 the final of the English Amateur Championship at Hunstanton had been decided by an impossible stymie at the 39th hole – the third extra hole played in the competition – and it was shortly after this that the stymie was abolished from golf.

The Crosby

The great entertainer Bing Crosby had a life-long passion for golf, and he was a decent player in his time. From 1937 he hosted his own pro-am tournament. The Crosby, as it is called, was played at Pebble Beach for many years.

Crosby was also one of only a handful of golfers to have scored a hole-in-one at the 16th on the exclusive Cypress Point course in California. When he died in 1977, it was just after he had completed a round of golf.

GOLF

The Old Course at St Andrews

Holes and championship lengths (2005).

1 *Burn* 376yds par 4
   The Swilcan Burn loops across in front of the green.

2 *Dyke* 453yds par 4
   The 'dyke' is the old wall which forms the
   boundary between the hotel and the 17th fairway.

3 *Cartgate* 397yds par 4
   Named because of its proximity to the cart track,
   which crossed the fairway and led to the beach.

4 *Ginger Beer* 480yds par 4
   The site where Old Daw Anderson set up his
   refreshment stall in the1850s, from which he
   reputedly sold more fortifying beverages in
   addition to ginger beer.

5 *Hole O'Cross* 568yds par 5
   This may have been the former site of a cross, or
   a reference to the gulley golfers had to cross to
   reach the green.

6 *Heathery* 412yds par 4
   A reminder of the times when the green was
   largely heather.

7 *High* 390yds par 4
Shell bunker is one of the largest traps on the course.

8 *Short* 175yds par 3
Self-evidently, the hole is named after its length, or comparative lack of it.

9 *End* 352yds par 4
The last 'out' hole on the course.

10 *Bobby Jones* 380yds par 4
Named after the celebrated golfer who died in 1971 and who had such a close association with St Andrews.

11 *High* 174yds par 3

12 *Heathery* 348yds par 4

13 *Hole O'Cross* 465yds par 4

14 *Long* 581yds par 5
This is the longest hole on the course.

15 *Cartgate* 456yds par 4

16 *Corner of the Dyke* 423yds par 4

17 *Road* 455yds par 4
Named after the turnpike road running behind the green, which has proved the downfall of many a top professional, most memorably when it cost Tom Watson the 1984 Open.

18 *Tom Morris* 357yds par 4
Tom Morris considered the18th green to be his finest work.

Links

'The grounds on which golf is played are called links, being the barren sandy soil from which the sea has retired in recent geological times. In their natural state links are covered with long, rank bent grass and gorse. Links are too barren for cultivation: but sheep, rabbits, geese and professionals pick up a precarious livelihood on them.'

Sir Walter Simpson

Historical Precedent

It is known that golf was played in St Andrews by the early 16th century. A charter in January 1552 confirms the rights of the town's citizens to use the now famous links for 'golf, futball, shuteing'. Golf may, however, have been played at St Andrews as far back as 1413 when the university was founded there.

Pot Luck

Early hole markers would sometimes be in the form of a wicker lobster pot attached to a cane – the idea being that, unlike a flag, the pot gave the golfer no clue as to the wind direction, thus making his task even more challenging.

Marx on Golf

Groucho Marx was an enthusiastic if somewhat erratic golfer. He once hit a hole-in-one at the Brae Burn Country Club near Boston and was photographed the following day by a local paper with the great Bobby Jones and Walter Hagen. The caption ran: 'Groucho Joins the Immortals'.

With more bravery than sense, Groucho agreed to re-play the hole the next day for the benefit of the press – and under the glare of publicity completed it in 22 shots. The next day the newspaper that had trumpeted his achievement ran another headline: 'Groucho Leaves The Immortals'.

Cricket's Loss

Henry Cotton, the great British player born in 1907, had been a better cricketer than golfer, but he was banned from cricket by his head master at Alleyn's

School for refusing a caning. Instead, the young Cotton concentrated on his golf swing and so successfully that by the age of 16 he turned professional. Cotton went on to win three British Opens. Though knighted in 1987, Cotton died before the title was officially bestowed on him.

British Open

Fourteen golf courses have hosted the Open Championships, one in Northern Ireland, the rest in Scotland and England.

Course	Open Championships
Prestwick	24
St Andrews	27
Muirfield	15
Royal St George's	13
Hoylake	11
Royal Lytham St Annes	10
Royal Birkdale	8
Royal Troon	8
Musselburgh	6
Carnoustie	7
Turnberry	3
Royal Cinque Ports	2
Royal Portrush	1
Prince's	1

Caddie Canny

'Remember the basic rule. Make friends with your caddie and the game will make friends with you. How true this is. It is easy to arrange that your guest opponent shall be deceived into undertipping his caddie at the end of the morning round, so that the news gets round among the club employees that your opponent is a no good, and the boys will gang up against him.'

Stephen Potter, *Golfmanship*

Dropped Balls

Sooner or later someone gets bored with conventional golf and feels the need to extend the scope of the game. This happened at the Westbury Golf Course in 1928 when teams competed to see who could drop a golf ball the closest to a hole from their aeroplane. A team captained by Willie Hammond reportedly won this bizarre contest by three holes.

Toogood to be True

The 1956 Tasmanian Open finished with an interesting trio leading the field and taking the honours that year. The winner was Peter Toogood. The runner-up was his father, Alfred Toogood, while brother John Toogood finished third.

GOLF

Long-John Diegel

Leo Diegel, who won back-to-back PGA
Championships in 1928 and 1929, used to enjoy
betting fellow golfers that he could shoot a round of
75 or under playing on just one leg. Many took up
his wager – and many lost.

A Double First

In 1904 W. J. Travis, who had been born in Australia
but was then a naturalised American, became the first
foreign player to win the British Amateur
Championship. This was not the only feature of his
victory that drew comment. Travis had won using a
centre-shafted Schenectady putter, which had never
been seen before in Britain. Clearly its arrival did not
please the golfing establishment, because centre-shafted
putters were soon declared illegal and their use was
prohibited for many years.

Lucky Strike?

Competing in the 1934 US Open, Bobby Cruickshank
could scarcely believe his luck when he was playing the
11th hole and saw his ball skip across a water hazard to
land safe and sound on the opposite side. Cruickshank
was so delighted that he tossed his club into the air,
overlooking the fact that what goes up must come

down. Unfortunately for him, when it did come down, the club landed squarely on his head and knocked him out cold. When he did recover his senses, Cruickshank continued the round feeling pretty groggy, but still came in a respectable third with a score of 76.

80 and Out

Richard Nixon's fall from grace as President of the United States did at least allow him to concentrate on his golf – and in 1978, four years after his removal from office, the 65-year-old Nixon broke 80 for the first time.

When he had been Vice-President to President Eisenhower in the 1950s, his golf-mad boss had criticised Nixon's lack of prowess on the course. So Nixon had concentrated on his game and made sufficient improvement to shoot a round of 84 – and beat Eisenhower at the same time.

Careless Talk

Careless talk can cost … well, golf matches. During the 1971 Ryder Cup fourball between Americans Arnold Palmer and Gardner Dickinson and Britain and Ireland pairing Bernard Gallacher and Peter Oosterhuis, Palmer hit a booming tee shot at the 7th. Gallacher's American caddie Jack McLeod instinctively cried out,

'Great shot, what did you hit?' To which Palmer equally instinctively replied, 'Five iron.'

Even though this was a purely innocent exchange, McLeod had technically broken the rules by apparently asking his opponents for advice. So the referee had to award the hole to Palmer and Dickinson.

Golf Down Under

Before it was destroyed by fire in 1948, the club house at the Sodom and Gomorrah Golf Club at Kallia, Israel, stood 387m (1,250ft) below sea level.

Mt Dundas Open

In August the Thule Army Base in Greenland stages one of the golf world's more bizarre annual tournaments. This is a nine-hole, par 36 competition played out on the icy, rocky flanks of Mt Dundas that stands overlooking the base. Those taking part first climb 720 feet up the mountain, where circles of rocks have been spray-painted green. In addition to carrying conventional golf clubs and balls, players are also required to carry a square of carpet to putt from. The reward for this gruelling challenge is a certificate, which reads:

Let it be known and made a matter of record that: on (date), (your name) did with reckless abandon and total disregard for life and limb, take golf club in hand and scale the treacherous heights of Mt Dundas and with a dazzling display of hooks, slices, bad bounces, aerial putts, profanity and lost golf balls, did participate in the annual Mt Dundas Open, the world's northernmost golf tournament (76° 32′ North Latitude). Let it also be known that this task of questionable sanity was accomplished despite near-freezing temperatures, numerous patches of casual Arctic water (snow drifts) and the threat of 18mph phase winds descending upon the participants with little warning. It is, therefore, with tears in our eyes and fear of certain retribution of Nanok of the North, that we the under-signed do hereby attest that this deed was truly done.

On Your Metal

Blacksmith Thomas Horsburgh experimented with making steel shafts for golf clubs as early as the 1890s. However, the first seamless steel-shafted clubs were not made in Britain until 1912. And they were regarded with some mistrust by purists in the early days. Nowadays, even many 'woods' are made of metal – hence the term 'metal woods'.

The Royal and Ancient only legalised clubs with steel shafts in 1929, nearly two decades after they were first produced. Even this belated recognition only came after the Prince of Wales – the future, ill-fated Edward VIII

– played with a set of the new clubs on the Old Course at St Andrews. The R & A could hardly disqualify the heir to the throne, so they legalised the clubs.

Billy Burke, who fittingly was a former ironworker, was the first player to win the US Open with a steel-shafted club when he took the title in Toledo, Ohio, in 1931.

Boomerang Ball

Playing at Shillinglee Park, in Surrey, in 1992, Robin Quantrill hit a 250-yard drive down the fairway only to see his ball land on a gang mower, which then made its way back up the course towards him until it reached the tee where he was standing.

A Putt wi' a Wedge

This was the airily dismissive description given by Hamilton 'Hammy' McInally, after he had won his semi-final match at the 1947 Scottish Amateur Championship, played at Glasgow Gailes.

McInally, who had formerly worked as a miner, had won two pre-war championships (in 1937 and 1939). A decade after his first victory he found himself in a very closely contested semi-final in which he was twice stymied by his opponent's ball blocking his line to the hole. On both occasions, McInally accomplished the remarkable feat of lofting his ball over that of his opponent and into the cup. Few disagreed that he deserved to win the match but when someone complimented him on his astonishing skill at the stymied holes, he replied nonchalantly, 'Och, it's nothing. Just a putt wi' a wedge.'

McInally was playing for Scotland once in the amateur home internationals at Hoylake and, to the satisfaction of the team captain, was leading by several holes at the turn of his singles match. Satisfied that that game was in the bag, the non-playing Scottish captain went off to see how his other players were faring. Some time later he was amazed to see McInally's match progressing down the 17th. Taking his player aside, the captain asked what had happened.

Indicating his opponent, McInally replied, 'I showed him where he was going wrong and now we are having a real fine game.'

Servant of Two Masters

'Hitting a golf ball and putting have nothing in common. They're two different games. You work all your life to perfect a repeating swing that will get you to the greens, and then you have to try to do something that is totally unrelated. There shouldn't be any cups, just flag sticks. And then the man who hit the most

fairways and greens and got closest to the pins would
be the tournament winner.'

Ben Hogan

Late Call

Playing close to the Arctic Circle doesn't have too
many advantages for a golfer, but at least you can finish
late in summer in the lands of the midnight sun. The
Arctic Open in Iceland was decided by a play-off in
1992, and was eventually won by Briton John
Drummond at 4.30am.

A Club for All Seasons

The Golf de Mont d'Arbois, in Megève, France,
transforms from being a golf course in summer to a ski
resort in winter.

Local Knowledge

'I never had any thought the whole week. I figured my
caddie [Jerry Beard] knew the course a lot better than
me, so I put out my hand and played whatever club he
put in it. I'd say, "How hard do I hit it?" He'd tell me
and I'd swing. The guys who come down here once a
year and try to get smart with Mr Jones' course are the
dumb ones.'

Fuzzy Zoeller, on winning the 1979 Masters as a rookie

Winning Shot

In 1987 Nick Faldo faced the last nine holes of the final round of the Open three shots behind the leader, Paul Azinger. Playing in front of Azinger, Faldo was desperate for a birdie to make up ground on the American. Although this eluded him, he continued to equal par on every green. Behind him Azinger dropped shots on both the 10th and 11th holes, leaving one shot separating him from Nick Faldo. Their scores stayed like this all the way to the 17th hole, where Faldo again equalled par. With the last hole to play, he hit a good drive off the tee and then faced a five-iron shot to the green, which he later described like this: 'And then comes this vital shot and you can't think about it. You have to hit it from memory. Then I had and it was straight on the flag, and I wanted to shout out "Cor, look at that." I went hot and cold all at the same time and then it was all over.'

As far as Nick Faldo was concerned, it almost was. With his final putt, Faldo set Azinger a target of 279, five under par for the tournament. At the same time, one hole behind, Azinger took six strokes to get out of trouble and this cost him the lead. With their scores tied, he needed a birdie to win the Open. But where Faldo's iron had served him so well on the hole, Azinger's let him down. He chose to drive from the tee with an iron and this left him too far from the hole to

overhaul Faldo whose nerve had held as his opponent
had faded down the back nine.

Victory or Death

Famous as the conclusion to the letter written by
Colonel William Barrett Travis, when the force he
commanded was surrounded by Mexican troops at the
Alamo, these words (in fact Travis's whole letter) were
read to the US Ryder Cup team by President George
W. Bush during the 1999 competition, after the second
day when they were losing 10–6. His timely
intervention evidently kindled something in his fellow
countrymen, who set to and won the trophy.

Design Courses

The first international conference on golf course design,
location and environment to be held in the United
Kingdom, was staged by the British Institute of Golf
Course Architects in the summer of 1992. When the
conference concluded a statement was issued, showing
that the demand for golf facilities remained strong
despite the recession of the early 1990s:

The conference delegates ... concluded that the
traditional figures used by the Sports Council to gauge
the level of provision needed – one course for every
35,000 people – is now seriously out of date and

instead called for a new benchmark figure of one course
for every 25,000 people to be adopted in order to cater
for growing demand. At least 1.7 million players
presently play on 1,700 courses, while demand for the
game has more than doubled in just 20 years. A
speaker informed the conference that, in recession-
struck 1990 alone there were over 1,000 applications
for golf courses throughout the United Kingdom.
William Hillary, senior partner in a firm of chartered
surveyors, pointed out that 170–200 acres are needed
for a typical golf course – more if extensive areas of
woodland or amenity land are included – and that the
successful application would be more than likely to
include a new clubhouse of 4,000–5,000 square feet;
double that for a well located major golf centre with
full retailing facilities.

Bunny Clubs

Until well into the 20th century the grazing of rabbits
was the principal means of keeping fairways tidy at
many golf courses.

A Curious Taste for Golf

Following the mysterious death of one of his cattle, a
German farmer asked his vet to conduct an autopsy,
which revealed a golf ball stuck in the cow's throat.
The farmer's land adjoined a golf course and he took

the owners to court claiming damages. Further investigation of the rest of his herd revealed that 30 of his cattle had developed a taste for golf balls and between them had 2,000 balls lodged in their stomachs.

Doing the Rounds

In 1998, a month after his 45th birthday, Sam Torrance played in the Trophée Lancôme and in so doing became the first golfer in European Tour history to compete in 600 tournaments. In achieving this landmark in his 28 years on the tour, Torrance had walked an estimated 14,000 miles, played in the region of 150,000 shots and had earned approximately £1,600 per round, or £22 per stroke.

Dealing with Dimples

By the early 1980s the average golf ball had 330 dimples in its cover. Twenty years later that number had increased to 415.

The normal depth of the dimples is 0.3mm. If they were just one tenth of this depth, the flight to 'first bounce', other factors being equal, is reckoned to be halved.

The dimpled surface of a golf ball also helps create backspin. This is reckoned to amount to 60 revolutions a second for a good tee shot. However, shots with a 9-iron can set up speeds of 170 revolutions per second. To put these statistics into perspective, golfers should remember that, in a 200-metre drive, the ball will travel one metre before it has completed one revolution.

All in the Family

Three generations of the Fribley family holed-in-one on the same course – and on the same hole. The first to achieve this feat on the 7th hole at the Pana Country Club course in Illinois was John Fribley in 1971. Four years after that, John's grandson Scott hit the spot. A full sixteen years later, John's son Joseph completed the unlikely trio.

Ryder Cup Seeds

In 1926 British seed merchant and passionate golfer, Samuel Ryder, watched an unofficial match between Britain and the US at Wentworth and came up with the idea for what became known as the Ryder Cup. Ryder had earned a fortune and established a sizeable business after another brainwave: selling seed in handy penny packets. However, the burden of work took its toll and he was advised to take up golf as a means of relaxing and taking exercise. Ryder presented a trophy for his proposed tournament and also funded the British team. The Ryder Cup was founded the following year,

in 1927, though Ryder himself saw only two of the
competitions named after him before his death in 1936.

Ryder had his own private nine-hole course at his home
in St Albans and engaged Abe Mitchell, one of the top
golfers in Britain at that time, to act as his professional.
Mitchell was the model for the golfer shown in the
address position on the top of the Ryder Cup trophy.

Ball Speed

Good golf shots can easily result in the ball moving
away from the club head with a velocity of 150 km/h
(95 mph). However, long-hitters are capable of
producing speeds of 250 km/h (160 mph).

Club Rules

From January 1938 the United States Golf Association
ruled that players should carry no more than 14 clubs
with them as they played. The Royal and Ancient
issued a similar edict in 1939. Before that, players had
so many different varieties of clubs to choose from, they
could carry 20 or more with them during a round.

Ian Woosnam's infamous mishap with the caddie who
left too many clubs in the bag – costing the Welsh
player a two-stroke penalty and quite possibly the 2001
Open – is not the only occasion on which a caddie has

cost a player dear. In 1946 Byron Nelson was heading
for the US Open title at the Canterbury Golf Club,
Ohio, when his caddie Eddie Martin kicked their ball
while clambering under a spectators' rope at the edge
of the fairway on the 15th. The blunder cost Nelson a
one-stroke penalty, and he eventually tied with Lloyd
Mangrum. Nelson lost the play-off.

And perhaps Woosnam should count himself lucky that
he lost only two shots. In the 1965 US Amateur
Championship Robert Dickson was penalised for
carrying one too many clubs in his bag. The club
wasn't actually his, and he hadn't used it, and he only
carried it around for a few holes. But still he was
penalised *four* shots – and missed winning the
championship by just one stroke.

Clever Shot

Sea captain Maitland Dougal came up with a neat
solution when he had to play in windy conditions in the
1860 Autumn Medal Competition at St Andrews.
Dougal, who had just spent five hours keeping his ship
off nearby rocks and so knew the strength of the wind,
drilled a hole in his ball and filled it with buckshot to
stop it being blown about. He finished second in the
competition.

GOLF

Boom Boom, Iceman and Friends

Like many well-known sports personalities golfers have collected nicknames down the years. Among them are:

Fred 'Boom Boom' Couples – a testament to his driving.

Ernie 'The Big Easy' Els – nothing to do with the American city of similar description (New Orleans), Els's tall stature and easygoing manner lend him a presence all of his own.

Sergio 'El Niño' Garcia – two possible meanings arise here. Garcia supposedly acquired his name from the Spanish for 'the boy'. Alternatively, the nickname could refer to the very stormy weather patterns that arise every few years, mimicking Garcia's talent for taking courses by storm.

Ben 'The Iceman' Hogan – seldom phased, Hogan's calm demeanour on the course always remained unruffled.

'Lord Byron' Nelson – Known as the 'Lord of the Links', Byron Nelson was truly one of the greats of the game of golf. His first name also had a convenient reference to the 19th-century romantic poet, Lord Byron.

Jack 'The Golden Bear' Nicklaus – blond and sturdy, Nicklaus merited his memorable name.

Greg 'The White Shark' Norman – Greg Norman greatly enjoyed deep-sea fishing, while his Australian accent and blond appearance reinforced the connection.

Corey 'Bulldog' Pavin – Pavin's fellow PGS player Mark O'Meara gave him this nickname because of Pavin's dogged persistence when playing in tournaments.

Craig 'The Walrus' Stadler – a name inspired by his solid build and walrus-like moustache.

Lee 'Supermex' Trevino – the nickname refers to his Mexican-American heritage.

Eldrick 'Tiger' Woods – Tiger's father gave his son the now-famous nickname after a Vietnamese soldier Woods Snr had befriended. His name was Nguyen 'Tiger' Phong.

Double Trouble

A double hole-in-one that wasn't happened at Royal Lytham and St Annes when David Senior landed his ball straight in the hole from the tee at the 15th. His partner Bill Lloyd smashed his own tee shot straight into the hole on the full, forcing Senior's ball out of the hole as well as his own. Senior's hole-in-one stood, but not Lloyd's.

GOLF

The Perfect Swing and How to Get It

All the important lessons of life are contained in the
three rules for achieving a perfect golf swing:

1. Keep your head down.
2. Follow through.
3. Be born with money.

P. J. O'Rourke

Old Masters

At the age of 73, the great Gene Sarazen managed a
hole-in-one at the 126-yard 8th hole – the par 3
Postage Stamp Hole – at Royal Troon. This was during
the 1973 British Open – and a full 41 years after
Sarazen had won the event.

Sam Snead's performance in finishing third in the
USPGA Championship in 1974 does not seem
remarkable – until you consider that he was 62 years
old at the time. It was an event that he had won some
32 years before. Snead's competitive edge hardly
seemed to fail as he got older. He won the Greater
Greensboro Open, a PGA event, in 1965 at the age of
52. Four years later he nearly took the Canadian Open
but got beaten in a play-off by Tommy Aaron. And he
was still able to shoot a round of 66 at the Quad Cities
Open in 1979.

Breaching Decorum

In the 1930s Gloria Minoprio used to compete in the English Ladies' Championship armed with just two clubs: a 3-iron, and a spare 3-iron. She never won the event.

However, Ms Minoprio did cause a stir in 1934 when she turned up for the Championship wearing, horror of horrors, trousers. Though stunning to neutral observers – especially men – Ms Minoprio's appearance scandalised the Ladies' Golf Union, which issued a statement deploring anyone who 'departs from the proper decorous costume of the traditional lady golfer'.

Sticklers for Detail

'Golf was invented by some Scotsman who hit a ball, with a stick, into a hole in the ground. The game today is exactly the same, except that it now takes some ninety-odd pages of small type to ensure that the ball is hit, with the stick, into the hole in the ground without cheating.'

A. S. Graham

Getting In on the Act

The comedian Bob Hope had a lifelong passion for golf and the Bob Hope Classic tournament is now a fixture on the PGA tour. As a player he played off a decent handicap of four at his best, and hit a number of holes-in-one. In 1949 he beat his friend and fellow golf fanatic Bing Crosby by two shots at the National Celebrities Tournament in Washington. Hope is reported as saying, 'Golf is my profession. I tell jokes to pay my green fees.'

The English-born comedian was awarded a medal by the PGA as 'one of the three men who have done the most for golf'.

By Battle, Stamp and Wildlife

The holes at the links course at Troon have some colourful names. The 8th is known as the Postage Stamp and is very short – just 126 yards, the shortest in British Open golf, while the 7th is called Tel-El-Kebir, after the name of a successful battle in Egypt fought on 13 September 1882, in which many Scottish troops took part. The 12th is known as the Fox because a copse once stood nearby in which foxes took shelter.

Hail to the Chief

Woodrow Wilson may have been one of America's most distinguished presidents, but he was one of the least able golfers among his presidential peers. This is explained in part by the fact that Wilson only took up the sport in his forties. Once bitten, however, he used to play constantly, often six days a week – and sometimes even used red balls to enable him to play in the snow. Wilson rarely scored below about 110, and once scored a 26 on a single hole at a course in Virginia.

Mr 55

In the round of a lifetime, the then university student, Homero Blancas hit an unbelievable 55 in a tournament, the Premier Invitational Tournament in Longview, Texas, in August 1962. This super-round on the par 70 course included 13 birdies and one eagle, and Blancas needed just 20 putts in all. Blancas, who also recorded a 62 on the same day and – unsurprisingly – won the event, turned professional in 1965.

Blancas ended his first year as a professional by winning the PGA Rookie of the Year award. He won four PGA events during his time on the tour and was placed in the top 10 of more than four dozen PGA tournaments.

In 1978, 'Mr 55' as he will always be remembered, was inducted into the Hall of Fame of his alma mater, the University of Houston.

GOLF

Air Shots

The law of averages suggests it had to happen some time – but you still have to feel sorry for what happened to Sharon Peachey at the 1980 Corfu International Championship. Her well-hit drive collided mid-air with a ball hit by another player on a different hole – and fell into a pond.

Catching the Bug

There was a huge explosion of interest in golf in the second half of the 19th century. This can be seen by some startling statistics. There were some 30 golf clubs in Scotland by 1864, and only three at the time in England. These were the Royal Blackheath, Westward Ho! and Old Manchester. Yet by 1900 there were about 2,300 clubs in Britain, with most of the new ones springing up in England. Many Scottish golf experts travelled around England at the time helping to design courses and teaching the game to hordes of enthusiastic devotees.

The massive increase in popularity of golf in late Victorian Britain was partly due to the growing prosperity of the middle classes at the time. With more leisure time on their hands people took holidays or short breaks, often imitating the Royal Family – who famously holidayed in Scotland. While on their visits, the English got to know golf, and gradually brought the game back home. Another key factor was the huge expansion of the railway system in late 19th-century Britain, which opened up parts of the country for the first time, including seaside resorts and also links golf courses.

Time Penalty

Players tackling the ninth hole on the Portal Golf Club in North America can find themselves taking as long as 65 minutes to complete it, even though the hole is only 125 yards long.

The reason? Geography. Not that there is a mountain to scale in this case. The tee is situated in the Canadian province of Saskatchewan, where daylight saving time is not observed. The green, however, lies across the 49th parallel in the US state of North Dakota, where daylight saving is observed. For six months every year, then, there is a one-hour time difference between the tee and the hole.

Towering Shot

Approaching the 18th hole on the final round of the Hawaii Open, the Japanese player Isao 'the Tower' Aoki hit his second shot and watched it land – still 90 yards short of the pin. This made it almost certain that

Jack Renner, who had already completed his final round, would win the tournament. However, Aoki was determined to have one final flourish. For this he chose his pitching wedge and sent his ball arcing towards the green, where it landed, rolled to the cup and plopped inside. With that sensational shot Aoki carded an eagle, beat Renner by one shot and became the first Japanese golfer to win on the US Tour.

Two for One

Jimmy Hines once earned himself and playing partner Sam Snead a birdie from the same shot. Hines was playing to the green during the USPGA at Shawnee in 1938. His chip shot cannoned into Snead's ball on the green, and both balls rolled unerringly into the hole.

Watch the Birdie

According to the oft-related story told by Ab Smith, the golfing term 'birdie' stemmed from a game he was playing at Atlantic City, New Jersey, in 1899:

The second hole was a par 4 about 350 yards long. I was playing in a three-ball match with George A. Crump and my brother William P. Smith ... I banged away with my second shot and my ball came to rest within six inches of the cup. I said, 'That was a bird of a shot and here I only get a paltry sum from each of you. Hereafter I suggest that when one of us plays a shot in one under par he receive double compensation ...' The other two agreed and we began right away to call it a 'birdie'.

To extend the analogy, 'eagles' and 'albatrosses' are rarer than the average 'birdie'.

Speeding Drivers

When swung by an accomplished golfer, a driver travels at a speed of around 101 mph.

On the Ball

The aptly-named John Ball is not well known these days but he was probably the greatest amateur player of his time. Born in Cheshire in 1862, Ball first played in the Open in 1878, aged just 15. Ball was beaten in a play-off for fourth position but was still given a small cash prize (probably a half-sovereign). In theory this meant Ball had compromised his position as an amateur from the start. But it was later ruled that the age limit for receiving prize money was 16. So as Ball had only been 15 when he received his cash, he was still classified as an amateur.

Between 1890 and 1912, Ball won the Amateur Championship a record eight times. In the course of achieving this remarkable feat, Ball reached the semi-finals 13 times and finished runner-up on two other occasions.

In 1890 Ball became the first person from outside Scotland to win the Open, when he took the title in Prestwick. That year he also took the Amateur title – the first player to achieve this double in the same year. He entered the Amateur Championship for the last time in 1821, when he was in his 59th year – and still managed to reach the fifth round.

Winner Takes All

Professional golfers are usually rewarded with handsome financial prizes for winning golf tournaments, but this isn't necessarily the case, as a few examples show.

Bobby Jones was an amateur player and therefore out of the running for cash prizes. However, he was once rewarded with the gift of a gun for winning his division of the 1933 Savanah Open.

In 1955 Gene Littler was paid in silver dollars at the Las Vegas Tournament of Champions.

Lee Trevino won a jewel-inlaid dagger at the Moroccan Grand Prix Pro-Am.

Ian Baker-Finch won a cow in the 1988 Bridgestone/Aso (Japan) Open; although he did sell back the cow in exchange for $5,000.

Heading the list, of course, is Willie Park, who won the famous Moroccan leather belt after his victory in the inaugural British Open in 1860.

Lightning Lee

'There was a thunderous crack like cannon fire and suddenly I was lifted a foot and a half off the ground. "Damn," I thought to myself, "this is a helluva penalty for slow play."'

> Lee Trevino, on being struck by lightning while competing in the Western Open in 1975

Follow the Sun

Ben Hogan was more than just a supremely talented player, he was also a remarkably determined human being. This was shown in 1949 when the American, who at 36 was at the peak of his powers and had won the US Open the year before, was involved in a serious car accident in Texas. Hogan nearly died and was very badly injured. But not only did Hogan recover, he painstakingly rebuilt his shattered body and within 18 months was able to take the 1950 US Open at Merion – to huge public acclaim.

A film was later made about Hogan's life. Called *Follow The Sun*, it starred Glenn Ford as Hogan.

Statistics can tell you Anything

A survey conducted by the National Golf Foundation in the USA revealed that 22 per cent of golfers say they regularly score better than 90. Broken down between the sexes, that figure equates to 25 per cent of male golfers who make the claim and just seven per cent of women golfers.

Furthermore, six per cent of all male golfers say that they regularly break 80, while only one per cent of women golfers are bold enough to make that claim.

Age Reduction

In theory it gets a little easier for golfers to shoot under their age as they get older. But George Smith achieved the amazing feat of going round in 15 fewer strokes than his age at the Cypress Lake Golf Club in Florida in 1988. The 90-year-old shot an incredible 75. A few years earlier, in 1984, 84-year-old Charlie Law had managed to hit a 75 at the Hayston Golf Course, near Glasgow.

However, both of them must surely doff their hats to Henry George 'Dads' Miller of Anaheim, California, who shot 99 on a 5,734-yard municipal course. Miller was 100 years old at the time and therefore broke his age by one stroke. Dads, who only started playing golf seriously when he was 67, had previously shot an 82 at the age of 95.

Double Hat-tricks

Between 1877 and 1882, just two players won the Open, each winning the title three times in a row. The first was Jamie Anderson who won it at Royal Musselburgh in 1877, Prestwick in 1878 and St Andrews in 1879. The second was Bob Ferguson who won in 1880, 1881 and 1882 at the same venues and in the same order.

Beginner's Luck

Amateur player Gordon Taylor must have thought holes-in-one were not that difficult when he managed one at the Royal Dornoch Golf Course in Cape Town in 1906. However, it took him another 55 years before he achieved his second one, at the Royal Cape Golf Course.

Player of the Century

When Jack Nicklaus won the US Amateur title in 1959 at the age of 19, it was the first major win in what was to be one of the most remarkable golfing careers the sport has seen. Nicklaus took part in a total of 100 major championships, and finished in the top three in nearly half of them – 45. He won 18 majors, including the US Masters six times. His sixth win came in 1986 when he was aged 46. It is little wonder that in 1988 he was voted Player of the Century.

The Babe

Babe Zaharias was one of the stars of women's golf in the 1940s, winning a staggering 17 tournaments in a row in 1946/47 alone. But she was also an amazingly talented competitor in many other sports. She was a top-class baseball player and was nicknamed 'The Babe' – after Babe Ruth – when she hit five home runs in one game. In 1931 she broke four world records in track and field events, and in the Olympic Games that year won in the javelin, 80m hurdles and the high jump. She was however disqualified from the high jump for having used the Western Roll jumping technique – which was deemed 'unladylike'. Zaharias, who was born Mildred Didriksen, also excelled at basketball, billiards, hurdling, tennis and diving. It was during the 1932 Los Angeles Games that American sports writer Grantland Rice persuaded Zaharias – who was still only 18 – to take up golf. She was still winning tournaments in 1955, but died from cancer the following year – the end of a remarkable sporting life.

Golfing Dictionary

Address	Position a player adopts before playing a shot.
Air shot	A swing that misses the ball completely but still counts on the scorecard.
Apron	Area just in front of the green.
Back door	Movement of the ball into the hole, when it passes around the lip of the cup and drops in from the back end.
Back nine	The homeward (return) holes of a golf course.
Better ball	The best score of the two players playing as a team in a fourball competition.
Borrow	The degree to which a putt needs to veer from the direct line to the hole in order to compensate for the slope of the green.
Carry	The distance from where the ball is hit to where is first lands.
Casual water	Standing water on a golf course which does not form part of a hazard.
Choke down	To adopt a lower grip on a club in order to achieve greater control of a shot.
Cut	The stage in a competition, usually at the half-way point, when the competitors are divided into those remaining and those who must quit the tournament.
Dogleg	A hole that changes direction during its course.

Downhill lie	A position where a ball comes to rest on a slope running downhill towards the target.
Draw	A shot hit deliberately high that curves to the left (when played by a right-handed golfer).
Fade	A shot hit deliberately high that curves to the right (when played by a right-handed golfer).
Fore!	A warning shouted to other golfers that a shot is heading in their direction. It is common for the warning to carry an indication of the direction of the shot, such as 'Fore left!' The term is a contraction of a warning 'Beware before!' which was shouted to warn troops in the front ranks of a battle formation that cannonballs were being fired over their heads towards the enemy opposite.
Front nine	The opening (outward) nine holes of a golf course.
Gimme	A simple putt conceded in a matchplay competition.
Gross	The total score before the handicap is deducted.
Handicap	The system that allows players of differing abilities to play golf against each other on equal terms. Better players have

	lower handicaps; less proficient players higher ones.
Honour	The player who tees off first. This is usually the winner of the previous hole.
Hook	A mishit shot which curves violently to the left (when struck by a right-handed golfer).
Lag	To play a putt deliberately in such a way that the ball stops near the hole, but short of it.
Lie	Position in which a ball stops after a stroke.
Loft	The angled face of a golf club.
Long iron	Irons numbered 1, 2, 3 and 4.
Matchplay	A type of competition in which a game of golf is decided by the number of holes that are won and lost.
Mid-irons	Irons numbered 5, 6 and 7.
Mulligan	A second chance to strike the ball off the first tee, if allowed by the other players.
Pin-high	A shot that travels the distance between the player and the pin.
Pitch-lifted	A shot hit high from green to the pin.
Pitch mark	Mark left by a ball when it lands on a green.
Preferred lies	Regulation permitting the lifting of a ball during play, normally relating to wet or winter conditions.
Pull	A mishit shot that travels in a straight

	line to the right (when played by a right-handed golfer).
Push	A mishit shot that travels in a straight line to the left (when played by a right-handed golfer).
Rabbit	A novice or poor golfer.
Scratch	Term used to describe a player with a handicap of zero.
Shank	Mishit shot in which the ball is struck by the hosel (the socket of the club head into which the shaft slots). As a result, the ball usually flies off in completely the wrong direction.
Short iron	Irons numbered 8 and 9, and all wedges.
Slice	Mishit shot that curves violently to the right (when played by a right-handed golfer).
Strokeplay	A type of competition in which a game of golf is decided by the number of strokes played.
Sweet spot	The area of the club face with the perfect hitting spot.
Topped	Description of a mishit shot that runs along the ground.
Uphill lie	A position where a ball comes to rest on a slope running uphill towards the target.
Yips	A nervous state that prevents a player from putting normally. German golfer Bernhard Langer has suffered more than

most top players from the yips. In 1980 he helped overcome the affliction for a while when he bought a second hand woman's putter called an Acushnet Bulls Eye for just £5. That season he won the Dunlop Masters.

Not Seeing the Wood for the Trees

Poor Australian player Brett Ogle certainly saw rather too much of the trees in the 1990 Australian Open at Sydney. He was only one shot off the lead on the 17th hole when an unfortunate shot put him in the woods. All was not lost if only he could play his way out of the woodland. But unfortunately his next shot smashed into a tree, flew straight back at Ogle and struck him sharply on the knee. It is hard to know which was worse – the two-shot penalty for being hit by his own ball, failing to get onto the fairway, or the terrible pain of the blow on the knee. Ogle played on after medical treatment but his nine shots on the hole blew any chances of a win.

Presidential Power

Gerald Ford was a very keen golfer both before and after he became US President in 1974. Ford had been a powerful athlete, an American football player, and this was reflected in his golf. He once out-drove playing

partners Arnold Palmer and Gary Palmer – no mean
feat. He also made three holes-in-one and his best
round was 81.

However, his power was not generally matched by his
accuracy, and he did develop a reputation for hitting
the occasional spectator. It was fellow golf enthusiast
Bob Hope who quipped that, 'Gerald Ford made golf a
contact sport.'

18th-century Golf Clubs

Although golf was played in a number of places well
before the 18th century, the earliest written records
indicate that these clubs were the first to come into
existence.

Royal Burgess Golf Society	1735
Honourable Company of Edinburgh Golfers	1744
Royal and Ancient Golf Club of St Andrews	1754
Bruntsfield Links	1761
Royal Musselburgh	1774
Royal Aberdeen	1780
Crail	1786
Glasgow	1787
Royal Blackheath	1787
Dunbar	1794
Burntisland	1797

The Olympic Family

America's first female Olympic champion was a golfer –
a Chicago society woman named Margaret Abbott.
Only she never knew it. She captured the women's
Olympic golf championship in 1900 – the one time
women's golf was included in the Games. The event
was billed as 'The International Golf Competition at
Compiègne in connection with the Paris Exhibition',
and Abbott won just a silver bowl, not a gold medal.
She died in 1955 never realising she'd won an Olympic
title, thinking she had simply won just another
tournament like those she often entered back in the
States. Her mother Mary also competed in the event
and came joint seventh – the only time in Olympic
history mother and daughter have competed in the
same event.

Throwing in the Towel

Craig Stadler missed out on second place in the San
Diego Open at Torrey Pines in 1987 – thanks to a
towel. The player had hit one of his shots under a
bush and had to kneel on the ground to get at the
ball. Understandably anxious not to get his trousers
dirty, he knelt on an old towel that his caddie was
carrying – which was used to clean balls – and
executed the shot. Stadler quietly got on with his
round and forgot all about it – but alert television

viewers did not. Several phoned in – a trifle meanly one might think – to point out that the use of the towel was in effect building a stance – against the rules. Thus Stadler was disqualified for not putting the penalty in the score he signed.

Double Birdie

Some golf shots are almost too improbable to imagine – especially the freak ones that play to a golfer's advantage. Such was the case one day in 1928 when a Dr Alcorn hit an approach shot from one side of the fairway at a course in Australia. At the same time another player was making his shot from the other side of the fairway. Not only did the balls collide, they both plopped into the hole – earning each player a birdie.

Victorious Britons

Only three British players resident in Britain have ever won the US Open Championship. The first was Harry Vardon in 1900. He was followed in 1920 by Ted Ray, and fifty years later Tony Jacklin became the third in 1970, when he was the holder of the Open Championship title. In 1988 Nick Faldo tied with Curtis Strange for first place but lost the 18-hole play-off to his American rival.

However, in the first 25 years of the competition, British-born professionals who had emigrated to the United States dominated the US Open. Among them was Willie Anderson, who won the title four times, three of which were in consecutive years – 1903, 1904 and 1905 – a feat that has never been matched.

Championship Form

Althea Gibson is better known as the first African American to win a major tennis event, winning the Wimbledon and US titles in 1957 and 1958, but she also took up professional golf and played on the LPGA circuit from 1964.

Round in 50

In 1962, 72-year-old Chick Evans Jnr completed a goal he had set himself back in 1907, when he won his first US Amateur Championship. This inspired him to compete in the US Amateur Championships in all 50 states, a goal he accomplished 55 years later.

Members Only

Cypress Point Golf Club in southern California opened in 1928, and the stunning setting for the course was the idea of US Women's Amateur champion Marion Hollins, who together with local businesses paid

$175,000 for the 175-acre cliff-top site. An unusual feature for such a top course is that it has both consecutive par 3, and consecutive par 5 holes. The location in the foothills of the Santa Lucia Mountains, nestling next to the Pacific Ocean, makes it one of the most breathtaking courses in the world – but also one of the most exclusive. It has only 250 members, who guard their privacy closely.

Two-Chip Chen

This was the nickname given to the unfortunate T. C. Chen after his notorious final round at the 1985 US Open, which was held at Oakland Hills, Michigan. Chen was four strokes ahead of the field on the fifth hole, when he chipped onto the green but had the bad luck to hit the ball twice: once on impact and again on the follow-through. This cost him a two-stroke penalty. That fifth hole at Oakland Hills ended up costing Chen a quadruple-bogey eight and the tournament. He ended runner-up to Andy North.

Top Scorer

When *Golf Digest* sponsored a tournament for The Worst Avid Golfer it found a worthy champion in the person of Angelo Spagnolo. In the course of the competition he managed 66 on one par 3 hole and totalled 124 penalty strokes for his foursome during the round. After completing the 18-hole course, his score was an impressive – and unbeaten – 257.

The Old Guard

Before winning the first of his many golf titles in 1954, the great Arnold Palmer spent three years in the US Coast Guards. Palmer went on to become one of the sport's greats, his many feats including winning the US Masters four times. Palmer is often credited with helping the popularity of golf at the start of the modern television era. His frequent visits to the British Open in the 1960s – when he won it twice – also helped revive interest in the tournament among fellow American golfers and spectators.

Careful where you Tread

In the 1921 Open at St Andrews there was a tie for first place between Jock Hutchison, a Scot who had emigrated to the USA, and an amateur named Roger Wethered. In the third round, Wethered had been unlucky enough to tread on his ball while walking backwards to study the line of the shot, thereby incurring a penalty stroke. Without that penalty, the title would have been Wethered's – as it was, Hutchison went on to win that year.

GOLF

Now You See It, Now You Don't

Some players perform at their best under adverse conditions. When Jim England played nine holes in a blindfold and with only two clubs at the Chapparal Country Club in 1976, he managed a respectable 46. The next day England tried again, only this time without the blindfold and using a full set of clubs. He went round in 48.

In 1954 one Laddie Lucas achieved a round of 87 while playing blindfolded during a full 18 holes at the Sandy Lodge Golf Course in Hertfordshire.

Unique Hat-trick

The Open was largely ignored by American players during the 1950s, who preferred to play in the more lucrative US tournaments. The tournament was dominated instead by South Africans and Australians, who between them won the title ten times from 1949 to 1960.

Australian golfer Peter Thomson won the Open five times in all, including four times in five years between 1954 and 1958. Thomson was the only player in the 20th century to win the Open for three consecutive years, in 1954, 1955 and 1956.

Moonlight Serenade

Old Tom Morris took part in one of the more unusual games of golf seen at the famous old links course at Prestwick, where he was greenkeeper until 1864. During his last year in office, he set out at 11.00pm to play 12 holes of golf accompanied by Dr Knower, Major Crichton and Mr Hunter. The four of them began playing in pitch dark, though they knew the moon would rise at midnight. When they completed the final hole, only two balls had been lost: one each to the doctor and the major.

Golf on the Roof of the World

In the course of an expedition in the Himalayas, Captain F. E. S. Blair camped at a place where a short, bright green turf led to the edge of a lake. Describing the scene in his book *A Summer in High Asia*, Blair wrote, 'Being a golf enthusiast I had brought a driver and putter with me and, having made a hole in the short turf, I instituted a competition for the camp. I should think that this was the first time that the Royal game had been played at an elevation of upwards of 16,000 feet.'

Golf Tours

The modern form of golf was spread to Europe – and the rest of the world – largely thanks to travelling

Britons and in particular Scots. The first European club outside Britain is thought to be the Golf Club de Pau in south-west France, created by British visitors drawn to the area's glorious scenery in 1856. It's believed golf may have been played even earlier in the area, by Scottish officers serving with the Duke of Wellington's army in the Napoleonic wars.

Given a Good Stretch

Inside a golf ball, beneath its dimpled cover, is a thin rubber thread stretched to the length of a good tee shot: 255m (285yd). This stretched thread exerts a force on the inner core of a golf ball which is greater than the weight of a large car, and the energy packed into that stretched rubber thread is powerful enough to raise a man weighing 70kg (10st 10lb) 60cm (2ft) off the ground.

The first rubber core ball was patented in 1899 in the USA by Cobrun Haskell and Bertram Work, the latter working for the B. F. Goodrich Rubber Company in Ohio. Another Goodrich employee, J. Gammeter invented the first golf ball winding machine, that mechanised the whole manufacturing process, two years later. When the first Haskell balls arrived in Britain in 1901 they caused an immediate controversy. Not only did thy travel further than balls made from gutta percha, they were livelier on greens and they were also three times the price of the best gutta percha balls, which placed well-to-do golfers who could easily afford them at a distinct advantage over those of more restricted means. By the following year rubber core balls had been reduced in price: they were now only twice as expensive as those made from gutta percha.

All-American Golf

On 14 September 1963, Floyd Satterlee Rood teed off beside the Pacific Ocean on a round of golf that he had planned would take him right across America to the Atlantic on the other side of the country – hitting a golf ball all the way. A little over a year later, on 3 October 1964, he reached his destination having walked 3,397.7 miles, having played 114,737 strokes and having lost 3,511 balls along the way.

Ladies' Days

Women's golf was played in the second half of the 19th century, but in a restricted way. It was considered bad form for a woman golfer to raise the club above her shoulders, and the game for women was really just pitch and putt. The movement of the players was not helped either by the long, bulky skirts they had to wear while playing.

GOLF

The Rules of War

St Mellons Golf Club on the eastern edge of Cardiff
had only been open three years when war broke out in
1939. Realising that enemy air attacks would present
club members with further challenges on the course, the
secretary drafted particular rules to be in force for the
duration of the conflict. Many other golf clubs followed
the example, particularly those in areas that came
under regular aerial bombardment in the Midlands and
south of England.

1   Players are asked to collect bomb and shell
     splinters from fairways to save these causing
     damage to the mowers.

2   In competitions, during gunfire, or while the
     bombs are falling, players may take cover
     without penalty for ceasing play.

3   The positions of known delayed-action bombs
     are marked by red and white flags placed at
     reasonably, but not guaranteed, safe distances
     from the bombs.

4   Shell and/or bomb splinters on the green may
     be removed without penalty, on the fairways or
     in bunkers within a club's length of a ball that
     may be moved without penalty, and no penalty

shall be incurred if a ball is thereby caused to move accidentally.

5   A ball moved by enemy action may be replaced as near as possible to where it lay, or if lost or destroyed a ball may be dropped not nearer the hole without penalty.

6   A ball lying in any crater may be lifted and dropped not nearer the hole, preserving the lie to the hole, without penalty.

7   A player whose stroke is affected by the simultaneous explosion of a bomb or shell, or by machine gun fire, may play another ball from the same place. Penalty one stroke.

Teetering on the Brink

Many golfers know that feeling when they putt close to the hole: if they only wait long enough, the ball will eventually plop inside. This happened to South African Denis Watson during the US Open at Oakland Hills, when he made a 12-foot putt at the 8th. The ball stopped agonisingly right on the edge of the hole and Watson, as is only human, waited and waited. His patience was rewarded and after a full 25 seconds the ball did fall in. Unfortunately he had also exceeded the time limit on waiting – and incurred a two-shot penalty.

Had he just tapped the ball in, he would have only been one shot down. At the end of the tournament he was just one stroke behind the winner Andy North.

Golf Buggies

'So the British, of all ages, still walk the course. On trips to Florida or the American desert, they still marvel, or shudder, at the fleets of electric carts going off in the morning like the first assault wave at the Battle of El Alamein. It is unlikely, for some time, that a Briton will come across in his native land such a scorecard as Henry Longhurst rescued from a California club and cherished till the day he died. The last on its list of local rules printed the firm warning "A Player on Foot Has No Standing on the Course."'

Alistair Cooke

Player's Luck

Gary Player, the great South African player who won the first of his three Open titles in 1959, always wore black in his early days. He claimed that as the colour absorbed more sunlight, it made him stronger.

It was Player, an assiduous trainer on the practice field, who also coined the phrase much used by modern sportsmen: 'The more I practise, the luckier I get'.

The Hardest Shot

'The hardest shot is a mashie at 90 yards from the green where the ball has to be played against an oak tree, bounces back into a sand trap, hits a stone, bounces on the green, and then rolls into the cup. The shot is so difficult I have made it only once.'

Zeppo Marx

Young Tiger

According to Earl Woods, father of the golfing phenomenon that is Tiger Woods, his son knew how to swing a golf club before he could walk. Allowing for an understandable degree of paternal exaggeration, Woods Snr cannot have been that far from the truth. For the young Tiger was only three years old when he posted a score of 48 for nine holes of golf.

Legal Intervention

Golf is classified as a non-contact sport, but sometimes tempers can get out of hand. The Australian professional Norman Von Nida was involved in a fight with US Ryder Cup player Henry Ransom during the Lower Rio Grande Valley Open in 1948. The local sheriff had to pull the pair apart and Ransom was later disqualified from the tournament.

GOLF

The Hogan Slam

In 1953 Ben Hogan competed in the Open
Championship for the only time in his career and
emerged the winner at Carnoustie, by four strokes.
Prior to his victory he had also won the US Masters
and the US Open, making him the first, and to date
the only, player to win all three titles in the same year.

First of the Few

When the South African golf champion, Gary Player,
won the US Open in 1965 he became the first winner
who was neither American nor British. Player was also
the first non-American golfer to win the US Open since
the victory of British champion Ted Ray 45 years
earlier, in 1920.

Over 650 Metres per Minute

This was the astonishing rate at which a team of 48
players completed a round of the 18-hole, 6,500m long,
Kyalami golf course, near Johannesburg, South Africa,
on 23 February 1988. From teeing off at the first hole
to sinking the final putt on the 18th, the 48 of them
took just nine minutes 51 seconds. Even more
impressive, perhaps, are the facts that they achieved this
using only one ball and that the score for the round
was only 73!

Marathon Golf

In contrast to the rate of play above, the South African team competing in the first round of the 1972 World Cup held at the Royal Melbourne Golf Club, in Australia, took six hours 45 minutes to complete their fourball round in the stroke-play tournament.